TruthQuest

Survival Guide

D0483219

0-8054-2485-7

Published by Broadman & Holman Publishers,
Nashville, Tennessee

Dewey Decimal Classification: 248
Subject Heading: YOUTH—CHRISTIAN LIFE
Library of Congress Card Catalog Number: 2001043812

Unless otherwise stated all Scripture citation is from the New American Standard Bible, © the Lockman Foundation, 1960, 1962, 1963, 1968, 1971, 1972, 1973, 1975, 1977; used by permission. Other versions cited are NIV, the Holy Bible, New International Version, © 1973, 1978, 1984 by International Bible Society; NKJV, New King James Version, © 1979, 1980, 1982, Thomas Nelson, Inc., Publishers; and NLT, New Living Translation, © 1996, used by permission of Tyndale House Publishers, Inc., Wheaton, Illinois 60189, all rights reserved.

Library of Congress Cataloging-in-Publication Data
Keels, Steve.
TruthQuest survival guide : the quest
begins! / Steve Keels with Dan Vorm.
p. cm.
Summary: Explains the fundamental truths of being a
Christian, seeking to give readers confidence in sharing their
faith and tools for depending on the Word of God.
ISBN 0-8054-2485-7 (pbk.)
1. Christian life—Juvenile literature. 2. Conduct of life—
Juvenile literature. [1. Christian life. 2. Conduct of life.]
I. Vorm, Dan, 1960–. II. Title.

BV4501.3 .K44   2002
248.8'3—dc21

2001043812

3 4 5 6 7 8 9 10 06 05 04 03

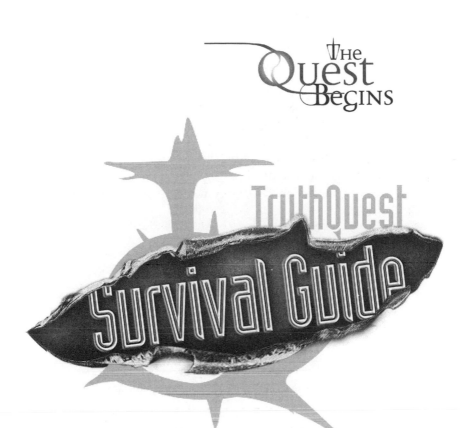

THE QUEST BEGINS

TruthQuest

Survival Guide

steve keeLs
with Dan vorm

BROADMAN
&HOLMAN
PUBLISHERS

Nashville, Tennessee

This book is dedicated to my good friend

MIKE PETERSEN

*who is truly the older brother I never had—
a man who appreciates my strengths and
has patience with my weaknesses.*

Contents

Acknowledgments / vi
Introduction / 1

Part 1: Proofs of God / 3

1. The Existence of God / 5
2. Why Doesn't God Show Himself? / 10
3. The Bible Is Reliable / 13
4. The Source of Evil / 18
5. Will the Real Jesus Please Stand Up? / 23

Part 2: The Character of God / 29

6. God Is Omnipresent / 31
7. God Is Omniscient / 36
8. God Is Omnipotent / 42
9. God Is Love / 48
10. God Is a Jealous God / 54
11. God Is All-Wise / 60
12. God Is the Trinity / 68

Part 3: The Essentials / 73

13. The Deity of Christ / 75
14. The Humanity of Christ / 81
15. Sin / 88
16. Justification / 94
17. The Cross / 100
18. The Resurrection / 107
19. Eternity / 114

Part 4: Experiencing God / 123

20. The Power of Friends / 125
21. How to Love Others / 131
22. Temptation / 136
23. The God Who Hears You (Prayer) / 141
24. Meditating on God's Word / 148
25. Church / 155
26. The Holy Spirit / 162

Notes / 168

Acknowledgments

I wish I could mention everyone who has had a significant part in shaping my life, and thus this project. However, there's only room to thank the following:

Dan Vorm, who made this book immeasurably easier by the use of his gifting and abilities. Aside from his writing and knowledge of the Word, he's a man of character who loves his family and is truly loyal.

Gary Terashita, one of the brightest men I've ever met; he is graciously demanding and a true friend.

David Shepherd, whose vision for TruthQuest continues to be an inspiration; he truly desires that these products get into the hands of students. I so appreciate our friendship, in spite of the miles between us.

John Thompson, whose love for the Lord, enthusiasm, and analytical eye has made TruthQuest what it is becoming today. Thanks for your heart for students as well.

Randy Alcorn, my friend and mentor, who will never fully realize how instrumental he has been in my life. (Randy, I'm not going to say anymore because you'll just start crying.)

Stu Weber, whose leadership style allowed the Student Ministry here at Good Shepherd the freedom to experiment, evolve, and thus impact thousands of lives. His love for Scripture and theology spurred many of the concepts behind this book.

The Student Ministry staff here at Good Shepherd over the years. The loyalty and camaraderie we've enjoyed as a team will never be forgotten. I'm so proud of all of you.

And most important, my precious family. To me, these are the most important people in the world. To my wife, Sue, my best friend and the love of my life. And to my children, who are my life; without each of them, my life would be empty.

Introduction

Why Take the Time to Read This Book?

This book is designed to help newer believers understand some of the basic things that are found in the Bible. If you read it carefully, you will begin to gain an accurate picture of who God is and what He's like. It's our desire that this book will help you build a strong, biblical foundation for your life. In so doing, you will protect yourself against error.

This book is not meant to replace your time spent reading the Bible, only to enhance it, by giving you insights that will help you in your own personal study of God's Word.

How to Use This Book?

This book is designed to be used in any of the following ways:

- *Personal study*—Read a chapter a day, writing notes in the margins if you'd like. It will be even better if you take the time to look up each Bible passage that is mentioned—that way you can see what is being said in its context.
- *Group Bible Study*—In a small group, have the leader read a whole chapter to the group while everyone else follows along; or you might want to take turns reading it out loud. Stop at significant points where people may want to talk about the stories or the Bible passages. After you've read the chapter together, spend time discussing the questions that are at each chapter's end.
- *One-on-one*—You can use this book with a friend who is a new believer, or even with a nonbeliever. Why not sit down over coffee and read through a chapter together. Ask your friend questions, such as "What do you think about this point?" or "Have you ever felt this way?" while referring to the content of the book. Use the questions at the end of each chapter to guide your discussion.

A Note Concerning the Stories in This Book

In order to make this book come alive, we have used a number of stories. You should know that the names have all been changed, as well as many of the key details. Each story is based on a true event, yet most have been disguised to avoid embarrassment or an unhealthy curiosity.

PART 1
Proofs of God

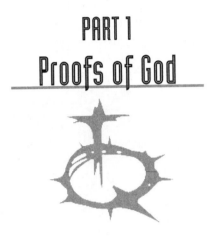

The Existence of God

Only fools say in their hearts, "There is no God."
Psalm 53:1 NLT

Phil sat in my office, concern written all over his face. An intelligent guy, he had lived for Christ throughout his high school years. His faith in the Bible had been strong, and everyone knew of his outspoken love for God.

Now that he had entered college, however, his once-strong faith was being shaken. Like a sandy shore eroded by a strong river current, Phil found that his simple faith in God appeared to be no match for the intellectual tide that threatened to sweep him away.

Through sobs he told me he now believed that the truths of the Bible were too simple in comparison to what he was learning at school. In particular, a professor of Phil's was challenging his beliefs, convincing him that the simple doctrines of the Bible were not enough to answer intellectual questions. Phil was beginning to doubt that the God of the Bible really exists. He was in trouble.

We sat and talked for a long time about the existence of God. Phil continued to pepper me with questions but found it hard to accept the Bible's straightforward answers. At the end of our conversation, I thought he might be willing and ready to understand that the professor was wrong in his assumptions.

CHAPTER 1

Then the real issue came to the surface—Phil's personal moral-ity. He told me of a certain girl with whom he was having a sex-ual relationship, and she was now pregnant. As he revealed his sin, it became clear that this was the root of his philosophical doubting. He could not justify his actions before God, so he felt he had to choose between giving up his sin or giving up his God. Apparently he chose to give up on God. Phil wanted to believe his professor to appease a guilty conscience.

One year after our discussion, my friend committed suicide. I can't help but think that his refusal to cry out to God in the dark-est moments of his life resulted in such tragedy.

Why Should Anyone Believe in God?

Since you have recently prayed to receive Christ into your life, your world is about to change (if it hasn't already). In Romans 12:2 the Bible says, "Don't copy the behavior and customs of this world, but let God transform you into a new person by changing the way you think. Then you will know what God wants you to do, and you will know how good and pleasing and perfect his will really is" (NLT). That means that Jesus is actually living inside of you by way of the Holy Spirit! He will now start to change your attitudes and actions from the inside out.

But remember, this is a process. It's kind of like growing an acorn into an oak tree—it doesn't happen overnight. In fact, if you're like most people, you'll even have some doubts and ques-tions along the way. Don't be scared of them. Instead, embrace them and count them as friends, allowing them to drive you into a deeper understanding of who God is and what He's like.

It may be that since you prayed to receive Christ many doubts have come into your mind about what you did. *What was that all about?* you may have thought to yourself. *I was sincere at the time, but now I'm even wondering if God exists.*

My son Daniel found himself in this type of situation recently. One of his favorite high school teachers would go out of his way to challenge Christianity and the Bible during class. Has that ever happened to you? This teacher would take pleasure in pointing out all the abuses of Christianity committed down through the centuries, therefore nullifying (in his mind) any reason to believe in the Bible. He was also quick to point out any alleged contradictions and historical inaccuracies. Never be fearful of these kinds of challenges!

Daniel could have been passive about this, but he wasn't. He decided to take the challenge and explore some answers. In a very respectful way he presented his findings to the teacher and the class. To his great disappointment, he found that the teacher refused to listen to him with an open mind. The teacher was content to hang on to his many misconceptions of what the Bible is all about.

So why should a person believe there is a God? What rational proof is there for His existence? If a nonchurched friend were to ask you those questions at school some day, would you know what to say? I believe there is convincing evidence that God exists, both from within us and in what we see around us.

First, instinct tells us there is a God. Ask any little child if God exists, and the answer will be a resounding "of course." It's not until someone works hard to "unconvince" us of God's existence that we really start to wonder. This instinct is a result of the fact that we are all made in the image of God. One writer in the Old Testament says that God "planted eternity in the human heart" (Ecclesiastes 3:11 NLT). In other words, we instinctively know that there is something beyond ourselves, and we're not talking about UFOs—we're talking about God! For this reason, those who are created want to find their Creator.

Second, every person has a built-in fear of the consequences that come from not following God. I see it every time I perform a funeral for unbelieving families; even godless people claim to be "religious" in some way or another. A man approached me at a funeral and said, "Pastor, my friend wasn't real religious, but I think he believed in God, and I'm the same way." Basically, this guy wanted me to comfort him because he was afraid of some possible consequences for not following his God-given instincts. People may live like they don't believe in

God, but often when faced with death they will acknowledge His existence.

There are many more reasons to believe that God is real than just those within us, however. God has revealed His presence by creating an incredible universe that has His "fingerprints" all over it.

Scientists often point to two principles of science, referred to as the first and second laws of thermodynamics. The first law tells us that matter cannot create itself—something caused it to come into existence.

Think of the house in which you live—the bedrooms, the bathrooms, the kitchen, etc. What did it take to make your house exist? It took a designer, a builder, a person with will and resources to make it happen. I'll bet you've never thought to yourself, *Wow, my house just evolved from nothing. How amazing!* We would never say something that sounds so dumb, yet when we talk about the world in which we live—a much more complex structure—we're taught that it came about by random chance.

Isn't it interesting that we so want to eliminate the existence of God that we are willing to develop an unnatural explanation to "substantiate" our views. Realistically, that's what evolution asks us to believe—it insists we throw common sense out the window.

I remember sitting in an astronomy class as a college student. The teacher was telling us that all of matter came from amino acids. Swirling around the ceiling were pictures of galaxies and stars and planetary systems—all colorful, beautiful, and complex.

I raised my hand and asked, "Where is God in all of this?" "He's not," came the reply, short and sweet.

I remember walking away from the classroom shaking my head in disbelief. Was I really supposed to believe that such wonderful design happened without a designer? Yet that is exactly what evolution asks us to believe. To me, that's a huge step of blind faith!

The second law of thermodynamics is often called the law of decay, meaning that everything in the universe is running down, that is, in a process of gradual disintegration.

For instance, think about the matter of chaos. Evolution teaches that everything around us is improving, moving from chaos to order. To me, this just doesn't make sense. Do you know of anything that ever changes from chaos to order on its own? As an exercise, take a sheet of paper and try listing all of the things you can think of that, by themselves, naturally move from chaos to order. On the other side, list whatever you can think of that naturally moves from order to chaos. I can tell you right now which page will be full and which will remain empty. A room doesn't clean itself (bummer!), a garden doesn't weed itself, and a universe doesn't order itself without some outside help.

No, don't let anyone convince you that science proves evolution and disproves the Bible.

Small Group Discussion

1. If you had to prove God's existence without the Bible, what would be your approach?

2. Why do people not want to believe in the existence of God? What do they fear?

Why Doesn't God Show Himself?

When I was a boy, I would lie in my backyard at night, look at the stars, and wonder to myself, *What's behind that star, and the star behind that, and even the star beyond that? And then, once you reach the final star, is that the edge of the universe, or does more stretch out beyond?*

I would always get so frustrated! I would think and look and think and look, until finally it felt as if my little head was going to blow up, so I'd just lie back and go to sleep! Yet behind those lame attempts at playing "junior astronomer" lay a very serious question: "I wonder if there is a God?"

To be honest, I didn't spend a lot of time wondering about God's existence—it was really nothing more than a nagging thought, a theoretical challenge about as important to me as solving the clues presented on "Jeopardy" each evening. It wasn't until after I prayed to receive Christ that I began to see God everywhere!

Now, as a believer, I can go to the ocean or stare at the mountains and be absolutely convinced of God's reality. It's only natural for me to see the wonder of His creation and say, "Wow, what an awesome God I serve." As an unbeliever, however, I used to see the same things and not even *think* about God—that was the natural thing for me to do before I committed my life to Christ.

I have had countless conversations with students as we've walked together at retreats along the Pacific coastline. Often I will be walking along the beach with a student who is yet to become a Christian, and I'll point out the beauty of the constellations above us or the vastness of the ocean before us.

CHAPTER 2

Doesn't it amaze you that God has created such endless variety on this planet? For instance, there are certain sea animals that live only in the deepest parts of the ocean, where no person has ever seen or probably will ever see them. Why is that? I think it is because God loves to display His infinite creativity. We can't help but be amazed at who He is when we think about these things.

"Oh my," I'll say to a student as we walk along the shore. "Look how God has revealed Himself. Look at the ocean; see how powerful God is, how awesome." Many times the student will look at me with a puzzled face; where I see God, he or she notices only crashing waves and sea foam.

Why is that? It's because the "natural man" (the non-Christian) cannot understand the things of God. First Corinthians 2:14 says, "But people who aren't Christians can't understand these truths from God's Spirit. It all sounds foolish to them because only those who have the Spirit can understand what the Spirit means" (NLT).

Now that you have trusted in Christ, God will begin to reveal Himself to you in many different ways. The Bible tells us that when we pray to receive Christ into our lives, He places the Holy Spirit inside of us. The Spirit then helps us to understand and see things about God that we never understood before.

There are many ways in which God constantly shows Himself to you and me. Three of the primary ways He does this are through His Word (the Bible), through His creation (everything you see around you), and through His people (everyone who truly has trusted Christ for salvation). If you spend time with each of these facets of God's revelation, keeping an open mind and heart, you'll soon find that any doubts about God's existence will evaporate away.

The answer to the question "Why doesn't God show Himself to us?" is that He *has* shown Himself—it's just that you may have missed seeing Him until now. It wasn't until you came to Christ that it became possible for you to see through the eyes of faith. Even now, many of your teachers and friends will wonder how you see Christ in His creation. You see Him because He is changing your heart as He lives inside of you. Remember the astronomy class I mentioned earlier? The professor knew far more about the universe and its design than I ever will. Yet he missed seeing the Creator—it was all simply information to him.

A classic illustration of "seeing and not seeing" is found in the Book of Exodus (chaps. 1–15) in the Bible. It tells the story of Moses and Pharaoh and how God delivered the nation of Israel from bondage. Both men saw the same plagues and the same miracles, yet Moses believed and humbled himself before God while Pharaoh hardened his heart and refused to believe.

Pharaoh saw the evidence, but he didn't see beyond the surface. Like my son Daniel's agnostic teacher, he discounted any rational arguments for God's existence based upon his own personal bias.

Moses and Pharaoh observed the same events: Moses saw God; Pharaoh chose not to. My son and his teacher wrestled with the same issues: one saw God; the other did not. When I stand at the ocean's edge with various students, I see God, but some of them see just the ocean.

The Bible makes it clear that every man or woman is without excuse when it comes to knowing if God exists or not. In the New Testament Book of Romans, God says, "From the time the world was created, people have seen the earth and sky and all that God made. They can clearly see his invisible qualities—his eternal power and divine nature. So they have no excuse whatsoever for not knowing God" (1:20 NLT).

God is real! The Bible says in Psalm 19:1 that the heavens and the Earth "are telling of the glory of God." Are you listening?

Small Group Discussion

1. What are the three primary ways by which God reveals Himself? What do we learn about God from each of these?

2. Do you agree that all persons will be "without excuse" when they stand before God? Explain your answer.

The Bible Is Reliable

Has a friend ever told you a lie?

If so, you know that it's something you don't soon forget. If it's a really good friend—especially your best friend—the pain is increased a hundred times.

Now answer this question: Do you believe that God would tell you a lie?

Take a minute to really think about this. Do you think it's possible that the God of the universe—the God who created you and everything around you—would ever tell you something that wasn't true?

This is a good question to ask ourselves because a whole lot depends upon our answer. If God *could* lie, then those of us who claim to believe in Him would be in serious trouble. We would have no idea which parts of the Bible are true and which parts were put there in order to mislead us.

In fact, if it were possible for God to not tell the truth, then we might as well forget about being a Christian and just live like our pagan friends. We could no longer have hope in eternal life, forgiveness of sins, or even the goodness of God.

The Christian life depends upon the fact that *God is truth* and that whatever He tells us in the Bible is completely reliable.

How Do You Know the Bible Is True?

As you know very well, there are many people who do not believe the Bible is the authoritative Word of God. Perhaps you are surrounded by parents, teachers, and

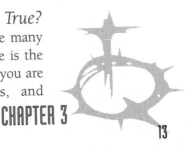

CHAPTER 3

friends who are directly opposed to the idea that the Bible is more than just another religious book.

How do you approach these people? Do you simply tell them to believe? To have "blind faith"? Faith is definitely involved, but sometimes people are surprised to find out that there are some good evidences that support the Bible's claim to be the "Word of God." Let's take a quick look at some of these evidences.

Changed Lives

A verse in the Bible says, "Faith comes by hearing, and hearing by the word of God" (Romans 10:17 NKJV). In other words, your faith in God and in His Word will increase as you give time to reading and studying what it contains.

There is a supernatural power connected to the reading of God's Word. If you really want your life to experience a true transformation, then you need to be reading the Bible on a consistent basis. Unlike other great literature, which comes from the minds of men, the Bible is intended to change your life, not just enlighten your intellect or entertain your mind.

Reading the Bible is different from reading any other book. That's because the Spirit of God, who was active in the writing of the Book through human agents, is active in every believer as he or she reads the words on the page. (Look up Hebrews 4:12.)

When you actively read the Word of God, you read the very words of the God of the universe for the express purpose of experiencing Him and being obedient to Him.

Evidence from the Bible Itself

When considering the validity of the Bible, it helps to understand what the Bible says about itself. There are two primary passages in the Bible that deal with this subject. The first one is found in 2 Timothy 3:16: "All Scripture is inspired by God and profitable for teaching, for reproof, for correction, for training in righteousness."

The word *inspired* in this verse literally means "God-breathed." All of the Bible, in other words, comes from God as if He had "breathed it out" from Himself. This means that the Scriptures are, in a real sense, an extension of God Himself—His character, His feelings, His emotions, His desires, His will. All of these things are conveyed to us through His Word.

The second passage is 2 Peter 1:20–21. These verses assure us that the Scriptures are not something put together by some holy men somewhere in a monastery. No, the Bible is not of human will but of men moved by the Holy Spirit. The Bible was written down on paper by various men throughout history, yet behind each of these men was God Himself, directing their thoughts, ideas, and words.

There is no doubt, due to these and many other passages, that the Bible claims to be of divine origin.

Evidence from the World

If the Bible is true, however, we would expect to see some kind of proof about its authenticity in the world in which we live. After all, many other books besides the Bible also claim to be the truth. So what are some "external evidences" that might confirm the Bible's claims?

First, there is the issue of archaeology. As you began to read the Bible for the first time, maybe you were surprised by the amount of history it contains. Both the Old and New Testaments are filled with references to cities, dates, nations, and events; in other words, the stories of the Bible all claim to be historically accurate. But are they?

As it turns out, archaeology has become the Bible's best friend. Throughout the past several centuries, archaeologists have shoveled dirt from many of the ancient sites mentioned in the Bible. Amazingly, no archaeological find has ever disproved even the smallest detail of what the Bible considers to be historical fact. According to Millar Burrows, a well-known archaeologist: "On the whole, however, archaeological work has unquestionably strengthened confidence in the reliability of the scriptural record. More than one archaeologist has found his respect for the Bible increased by the experience of excavation in Palestine."[1]

Another expert, W. F. Albright, had this to say: "There can be no doubt that archaeology has confirmed the substantial historicity of Old Testament tradition."[2]

Strong evidence for the Bible is also found in the area of prophecy. There are all kinds of prophetic predictions in the Bible: prophecies about the raising up and destruction of cities, about the land and people of Israel, and, of course, about the end of the world and the return of Jesus Christ. Amazingly, more than 75 percent of these predictions have already been fulfilled, the remaining ones having to do with the end times.

Although there are modern-day prophets who claim to know the future (i.e., Nostradamus or Jeanne Dixon), the difference between them and the Bible is that of accuracy. None of the Bible's predictions has ever failed, while secular prophets rarely get things right.

Particularly in one instance, the Bible's prophecies were so specific as to tell where a certain Person would be born, how He would die, the fact that He would be born of a virgin, and the kind of grave in which He would be buried. Only one life in all of history has fulfilled all of these circumstances exactly—the life lived by Jesus Christ.

A Warning

I have a friend, a young man who was raised in the Christian faith all of his childhood. When he was younger, he never doubted the Bible; after all, his parents believed it was true, and they lived their lives around that fact.

As Nathan got older, however, he began to doubt the fact that the Bible was true. Cautiously at first, like a person creeping onto thin ice, he began to question the foundations of his faith. "What if the Bible isn't true?" he asked himself and others who would listen. "Aren't there good reasons to doubt that it's really the Word of God?"

Over time Nathan became bold in his questions, to the point where he began to take more pleasure in asking the questions than in finding the answers. He worked hard to develop difficult questions, things that to him seemed unanswerable, holding these out as proof against the Bible's authenticity. When answers were given, he simply rejected them outright, revealing the fact that he wasn't on a search for truth, just a search for attention and rebellion.

He now delights in reading philosophical books and articles that are adamantly opposed to the Bible.

Don't be like Nathan. If you have questions, there are good answers available to help you understand any apparent difficulties or discrepancies contained in the Bible. Open your heart and be ready to meet with God as you read the pages of His Book.

Remember, He will never lie to you. Everything contained in the Bible is true. You can bet your future on it.

Small Group Discussion

1. How untruthful are people compared to God?

2. When was the last time someone lied to you? How much do you trust that same person today?

3. Since you believe God will not lie, then why is it so hard to sometimes trust what He says in His Bible? What kinds of things can help you begin to trust His Word?

The Source of Evil

The story on the TV news was almost more than any thinking person could handle. The anchorperson was telling how several little boys had pushed a five-year-old to his death off the roof of an inner-city apartment building. All because of a simple "I dare you."

It was one more tragic, senseless death in a world filled with question marks.

Although it took the news-anchor just fifteen seconds to relate the story, sandwiched somewhere between the sports and weather, it took me days and weeks to process the emotions that story stirred in my chest. I struggled with lingering questions: Why did it happen? Where were the parents at the time? How did the boys get onto the roof? What would make any kid do such a thing? And most important, where was God when that little five-year-old needed Him?

The Existence of Evil

Do you believe that evil exists? Of course you do—it's all around us. Even if you don't watch the news or read the newspaper often, there's no escaping the reach of evil's long tentacles throughout this world in which we live. Much of it seems distant from us, such as war or famine in faraway lands; the pictures may be real, but the faces are unfamiliar.

Yet evil strikes close to home too. Maybe you know someone who's been injured or has died in a car wreck. Or perhaps you have a parent who walked away from you and your family, leaving a hole in your heart that seems impossible to fill. Evil affects every one of us—no exceptions.

Evil is also something deep within us. Think for a second about those little boys on the roof. Did their parents teach them to do what they did? Of course not. No parent would be that stupid. Now think about yourself when you've done something wrong, such as tell a lie. Did your parents sit down and say, "Now Johnny or Susie, this is how you tell a lie and get away with it"? No way, your folks would never do that. You did it on your own.

Every time you do something wrong (the Bible calls this "sin") you confirm the fact that evil exists not only "out there" but also deep within your heart. All of us, by nature, have a built-in capacity for doing wrong. The Bible calls this our "sin nature."

Think of the most evil story that you have ever heard. We often hear people say, "If there is evil, then God can't exist, because a good God wouldn't create evil." To me, however, the fact that evil exists is consistent with what the Bible teaches us about the reality of evil. It says that

- God is not the source of evil, and
- He cannot be blamed for evil.

God Is Not the Source of Evil

So where did evil come from? If God is good, like the Bible says, then how did evil come to have such a grip upon this world in which we live?

The Bible says that evil originated with a person whose name is Lucifer. In the Old Testament Book of Isaiah, chapter 14, it says this about the once beautiful angel:

> "They will all respond and say to you,
> 'Even you have been made weak as we,
> You have become like us.
> 'Your pomp and the music of your harps
> Have been brought down to Sheol;
> Maggots are spread out *as your bed* beneath you,
> And worms are your covering.'
> "How you have fallen from heaven,

O star of the morning, son of the dawn!
You have been cut down to the earth,
You who have weakened the nations!
"But you said in your heart,
'I will ascend to heaven;
I will raise my throne above the stars of God,
And I will sit on the mount of assembly
In the recesses of the north.
'I will ascend above the heights of the clouds;
I will make myself like the Most High.'
"Nevertheless you will be thrust down to Sheol,
To the recesses of the pit."
(Isaiah 14:10–15; see also Ezekiel 28:14–17)

Lucifer, or Satan as he's called later in the Bible, is a created being who started out as the most beautiful of all the angels. His beauty went to his head, however, and he became prideful. Notice how many times the phrase *I will* is used in the above passage. In other words, Lucifer was all about his own will, not about God's will. It was because of this that God banished him from His presence.

We don't know how evil worked its way into Lucifer's heart; all we know is that pride consumed him until he set himself against everything that God is and does. God did not create evil, but He allowed for the possibility of evil by allowing His creature to freely love Him or deny Him. Satan was the first to choose against God, and one-third of the angels chose to rebel along with him (these angels are now called demons). Kicked out of heaven, these rebels will continue to fight against God until the day that Christ comes back in judgment.

Jesus talked about Satan (which means "adversary") in the most unflattering of terms. This is what Jesus said to some ungodly people in John 8:44: "You are of your father the devil, and you want to do the desires of your father. He was a murderer from the beginning, and does not stand in the truth, because there is no truth in him. Whenever he speaks a lie, he speaks from his own nature; for he is a liar, and the father of lies."

God Cannot Be Blamed for Evil

Have you ever wondered: "If God is good, then why did He create a world full of evil?" This question, perhaps more than any other, has made it difficult for some people to want to give their hearts to Christ. People often wonder if they can trust God if He is a God who can be blamed for the origin and existence of evil.

Let's explore this for a moment. Suppose you have a laptop in front of you right now. If your name is Justin and you want your laptop to love you, then just type in the words "Justin, I love you." Pretty cool, huh?

Actually, you can make your laptop say lots of nice things about you. How about "Justin, you are great" or "Justin, you're incredibly good looking!" How does that make you feel? Satisfied? Warm and fuzzy? Unless you're really weird, it probably doesn't do much for you. It's not the same as if your best friend or your parents were to tell you those things.

When God created us, He didn't want to create a bunch of robots (or laptops) that would only be able to act in a pro-grammed manner. He created us to love Him and follow Him out of our own free will. Without true choice, there is no true freedom.

John was a student who began his walk with God very well. He consistently came to youth group and church and was really growing in his relationship with God. Then he met a girl named Michelle, and his spiritual life began to go downhill.

John understood the biblical principles in regards to sexual temptation. In the beginning of their relationship, he and Michelle set up strict boundaries concerning physical touch, but over time those boundaries began to erode. Eventually they found themselves going beyond intimate conversation, and they started to compromise their morals by having sex together.

John felt horrible about it. He knew it was wrong, but he couldn't bring himself to stop. Each time he would go to be with Michelle he would ask God to stop him from committing sexual sin again, but when they were alone in a passionate situation, they would inevitably end up falling. John's response? He would blame God for not stopping him from committing the sin.

So here's the question: who is responsible for John's sin? Was God wrong in not preventing him from committing evil, or are John and Michelle responsible for their own choices?

Actually, this "blame game" has been around ever since sin first entered the world. Remember the story of Adam and Eve? If you were to read Genesis 1–3, you would see that Adam and Eve were created perfect but then chose to sin by eating from the only tree in the garden that God had told them not to touch. And when caught, what did they do? Eve blamed the serpent for deceiving her, while Adam blamed God for giving him such a ditsy wife!

To blame God is to sin against Him. Every time John blamed God, he didn't realize that he was sinning even more by essentially accusing God of being evil.

How should John have responded? First, he should have taken responsibility for his choices. God will help us when we ask, but He expects some effort from us as well. And second, John should never think that God would participate in evil by setting him up to fail. God takes no delight in sin. He cannot sin, nor does He ever tempt you or me in order to make us fail.

We are responsible for our own choices.

Small Group Discussion

1. Describe the most evil situation you have ever witnessed. Do you believe evil exists? Where did it come from? Who made evil?

2. Is God evil for allowing evil to exist?

3. How evil do you believe Satan truly is? What is he capable of doing with his evil? Should we fear his evil?

Will the Real Jesus Please Stand Up?

Four hundred freshmen packed the school auditorium as the vice principal positioned himself on stage behind the microphone.

"Let me talk a little bit about personal beliefs and how we should address them here at school," he began as the crowd of students quieted down to listen.

"We should be tolerant of each other here at school, especially when it comes to what we believe about religion," he continued. "We should all be respectful of one another and not say harsh things about another's religion. After all, whether you're a Mormon or a Christian, or whatever you believe, we all talk to the same God."

Suddenly a lone voice somewhere in the huge auditorium was heard before the speaker could begin his next sentence.

"That's not true," said the voice, not shrill or disrespectful, but bold and confident. Heads turned from every direction to see a girl who was now standing alone in the midst of her seated peers. "People can only come to God through Jesus."

As you picture this scene in your mind, hit the pause button for a moment. Look at the picture so far: hundreds of students, a typical assembly, a packed auditorium, and a statement from a vice principal that is totally false, even dangerous to the students' spiritual lives.

Now look at the girl who spoke: not a superstar or an attention-getter, and certainly not a student who is running for "Miss Popularity"; just a regular student who desires for people to know the truth.

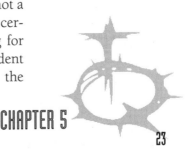

CHAPTER 5

Before we hit the play button, ask yourself this question: how convinced are *you* that Jesus is the only way to a relationship with God? Are you 100 percent convinced? Fifty percent? Ten percent? Or is the vice principal correct when he says that there are many ways to reach eternal life?

OK, now hit the play button in your mind. The stunned audience is silent as the girl sits back down. The vice principal stumbles over a few words, then goes on with his list of topics for the morning. Soon the bell rings and everyone stampedes for the door, making their way to the next class.

Nothing dramatic, really. The tense moment is quickly forgotten as school life continues uninterrupted. Behind her back, a few people make fun of the girl who stood up, but for the most part the whole scenario is no longer an issue.

The Incredible Name of Jesus

The point of the above true story is not that everyone should stand up in the middle of every assembly and challenge every bad statement. No, the point of the story is this: a young student believed so strongly that Jesus is the only way to God that she did not hesitate to stand up and make the truth known. No one would stand up like that for something she only believes in halfway.

Read what the Bible says about Jesus in Acts 4:12.

Many people have the view that there are many roads to heaven—that all religions are basically the same. The Bible teaches us something very different; in fact, it is quite exclusive. Jesus will not share the throne with Muhammad, or Buddha, or even Shirley MacLaine and the New Age movement. In fact, those who try to raise others up to Jesus' level are condemned! There is no other way to the Father than through Jesus Christ. (Read 1 Timothy 2:5–6.)

How does that make you feel when you hear about such a narrow way? Many people feel frustrated and angry when they hear this; they are afraid that God is somehow being unfair, that He is not tolerant enough with those of other religions. "I thought God was a God of love," they say. "How could God create such a narrow way, thus excluding so many sincere people of other religions?"

Several facts help us see that Jesus is the only way to God.

First, He is the only religious leader who is still alive; Muhammad, Buddha, Joseph Smith, and others are dead. They are in a tomb somewhere, and have been for hundreds, maybe thousands, of years.

But Jesus is alive. He rose from the dead, and for this reason God draws people to Him who also desire to be raised from death to life. Why would God draw people to someone who is dead? It wouldn't make sense. No, Jesus is alive today, living with the Father in heavenly glory.

Second, Jesus is the only man who ever lived who is completely sinless. Can you imagine making it through a day, a week, or even a month without doing anything wrong? No sinful thoughts, no selfish motives—none? Now imagine living a whole life that way. For you and me it is quite impossible, as it was for Muhammad and Buddha. It was not impossible for Jesus however. (Look up Hebrews 4:15.)

Though He is fully God, Jesus is also the only perfect human being who ever lived. As a man, He can fully relate to the things with which we struggle. He faced every temptation that we will ever face (and probably many more), yet He never gave in to those temptations. Because of this, He can sympathize with us in our temptations while also providing a way for us to overcome our natural inclinations to go against God.

The reality is this: people can have a religious experience following any kind of spiritual leader, but only through Jesus can a person have a personal relationship with the Father. This is because Jesus is alive today, and because He lived a sinless life. (Look up 2 Corinthians 5:21.)

Don't Settle for Less

Tom visited his former pastor, whom he had not seen for many years. In high school, Tom had been part of the youth ministry, though a real loner with few solid friends. Now, at the pastor's doorstep, he was obviously excited to explain how his life was changing for the better.

"Pastor, I just want you to know that I've been doing very well with the Lord," he said. "I met a girl, and she introduced me to the Mormon church, and now I'm really walking with God." Tom had come from a rough home, and he was very lonely while growing up. He had always wanted something that would bring him a sense of security. As he fell in love with this girl, he also fell in love with the love and acceptance he experienced as he spent time with her family.

The pastor was glad that Tom was happy, but he had to tell him the truth about what he was being taught. As wonderful and nice as his girlfriend and her family were, they were introducing Tom to a false Jesus—a Jesus who is very different from the Jesus of the Bible. No matter how good he sounds, a false Jesus is no more able to save a person than no Jesus at all.

"Tom, you tell me that you're walking with Jesus," said the pastor, "but in reality you're not walking with Him at all."

"Yes, I am," he resisted.

"No, you're not," the pastor continued. "You are having a religious experience, but you're not experiencing the Jesus of the Bible—the only true Jesus who can save us from our sins. The Mormon's Jesus is a created being, not the eternal God of the Bible who is equal to the Father."

Look up Galatians 1:8–9. You may have friends who are Mormons or Jehovah's Witnesses; be aware that the Jesus they are teaching is not the Jesus of the Bible. A different gospel can make a person feel good, have a good family, even enjoy life and have lots of friends. But in terms of a relationship with the true and living God, it doesn't work. Only the Jesus of the Bible has the power to save us from our sins.

When it comes to the issue of getting to heaven, the Bible clearly states that there is only one way—through Jesus Christ. As Jesus says in John 14:6: "I am the way, and the truth, and the life; no one comes to the Father, but through Me."

Small Group Discussion

1. Is God being a bigot by allowing people to be saved only through the person of Christ?

2. Why is it important that Jesus be the only way for salvation?

3. What if a religion teaches people to believe in Jesus, just not the Jesus of the Bible? Is it OK to put your trust in a false Jesus who is not fully God and fully man?

PART 2
The Character of God

God Is Omnipresent

Everyone in the youth group knew Kim. She was a strong believer, a student leader, and a girl full of convictions about how to live the Christian life.

She was also quickly becoming a phony.

In the secret places of her heart—where only God could see what was stirring—Kim began to pull away from the God of the universe. Though she at one time had held a leadership position in her youth group at church, over time she began to fall away. It was completely indiscernible at first—an occasional missed meeting, an ignored Bible study, a change of close friends from Christian to non-Christian.

When Kim noticed the fact that she was distancing herself from the things of God, she chose not to correct her free fall. Instead, she began to avoid kids from church. She'd hide behind her locker or bury her head in a magazine in the library—anything to keep from being asked why she wasn't showing up at youth group. Somehow she thought that if she could avoid these friends, she could avoid looking at the coldness in her own heart.

As time progressed, she became negative about the church in order to justify not going anymore. It was almost as if she thought she could fool God—that if she didn't show up at church, then God would be fooled just like the rest of her church-going friends.

In essence, Kim was trying to avoid the presence of God.

Adam and Eve had the same problem. After they sinned, they tried to hide from

CHAPTER 6

God because they were ashamed. They did not truly believe that God was everywhere, so they tried to run from His presence. They wanted to hold a secret from God, hoping He wouldn't become aware of what they had done.

The same is true today. Many people believe that they can run from God's presence. What they don't know is that God is everywhere—it's impossible to find a place where God cannot see you. This can be comforting if you *want* to find Him, but very frustrating if you're trying to escape His notice!

So just where is God anyway? Let's look at several things we can learn from the Bible.

God is in heaven. Though there is some debate about where heaven is located, we do know that it is a place of incredible beauty and unapproachable light. In the Bible, it is known as a place where God and His angels dwell. (Read Ecclesiastes 5:2.)

God is not bound by the universe as we know it. He dwells outside of space and time. If you were to travel to the furthermost star in the farthest galaxy of the universe, God would be there and beyond. He is infinite, which means He has no beginning and no end. He has always existed, and everything that we see around us, including time itself, was created by Him.

God will one day be present in hell. Those who reject Christ and the light He has given to them will experience an eternity of God's wrath. They will be forever paying the debt of their own sins instead of taking the free gift of Christ's having paid it for them on the cross. Yet even in that lonely, painful existence, God is there.

God exists in the tiniest of the elements. Think of one of the smallest building blocks of the physical universe—atoms. God is even there, at the atomic level. (Read Colossians 1:17 and Psalm 139:7–12.)

The Activity of God

Have you ever thought about where God exists all at the same time? Here are several examples.

- God is active in every nation.
- God is active in the depths of the ocean.

- God is active in the middle of the desert where no man exists.
- God is active in the North Pole where only animals roam.
- God is active in the depths of the universe where no man will ever explore.
- God is active in your life every second of every day, whether you think about Him or not. Imagine all of the hours, minutes, and seconds that pass by each day when you give no thought to His existence. Even so, He never leaves you or deserts you.
- God is present in the lives of unbelievers, even those who say they hate God. Imagine a guy who says he hates God; he ranks on both the Bible and on Christians, and he loves to debate with people by saying that God doesn't exist. Yet when he gets in his car alone after the debate, he isn't really alone at all—God is there. When he is in his room, there is God. When he sleeps at night, there is God. This guy can never escape the presence of God.
- God is present when evil takes place, though He is not the cause of evil. Think about someone who has done horrible crimes, such as a mass murderer or a serial killer. It may be that such a person has never been caught. No one knows who he is, why he did it, what were all the circumstances involved, etc.—no one, that is, except for that person and God. The killer who has escaped arrest thinks to himself, *No one knows; no one was there.* Wrong! God was there, and He saw everything that went on in that twisted scenario. In fact, someday God will bring that person to true justice, even if he escapes it on this earth—all because God is everywhere and He sees everything.
- God is in the past, the present, and the future because He is not bound by time. That's an amazing thought, one that is almost beyond our comprehension. Yet it's true.

If God Is Everywhere, Why Don't We Act Like It?

Now that you've given your life to Christ, your number one priority should be that of getting to know the God of the universe.

Not just intellectually, as you would study for an exam. No, knowing God requires that we focus on the fact that He is with us every moment of every day.

To be honest, though, there may be times when we'd rather not have Him watching what we do. Our fleshly nature would like it better if God were like a genie in a bottle—a magical spirit who would come running each time we had a wish, but who otherwise would leave us alone.

When we sin, we usually forget about God. Sin has a way of filling up our thoughts so completely that we forget that God even exists. That's what happened to a student named Nick every time he and his girlfriend would step over the line sexually. Nick and Jody would regularly go to church and actively participate in a Bible study. Amazingly, on many occasions they'd be in his car just ten minutes later kissing and fondling each other sexually, forgetting that the God they were just studying about was right there in the car with them.

If Nick and Jody would have taken a moment to say to each other, "We know God is here with us," then they probably would have been embarrassed and stopped their immoral behavior. To forget that God is always present is to open ourselves up to sin.

On the other hand, a young man named Troy tries to focus on God's presence every time he is alone in his car. He puts in some worship CDs and breaks out into singing and praise, not even caring what those in the lane next to him must be thinking. Troy knows that he doesn't have to go to a building or a temple in order to communicate with the living God. He understands that God is not confined to a place; He is always with Troy wherever he goes.

Sometimes Troy even gets in his car and goes for a drive for the sole purpose of spending time alone with the Savior. Sounds kind of crazy, but it works for Troy. It works because God is omnipresent—He is always available, always ready for you to call on Him, worship Him, pray to Him, and enjoy His presence.

Spend time focusing on the God who is with you everywhere you go. Find some good worship music and play it in your car or in your room as you study. Leave your Bible on your bed so that you're constantly reminded to spend time with Him, or better yet, get a small pocket Bible and carry it wherever you go. Do whatever it takes to fill your gaze with God.

Remember, He is "a friend who sticks closer than a brother" (Proverbs 18:24).

Small Group Discussion

1. List some practical ways by which you can practice the presence of God in every type of situation. Start with the most difficult situations.

2. Do you believe that sin can make people forget the presence of God? If so, give an example.

God Is Omniscient

Some people just seem to know everything.

Like the guy or girl in class who gets an *A* on a test after studying for thirty minutes, while you study for three hours and get a *B-*.

You know the type of person—always sitting at a computer, day and night, absorbing information like a sponge. Some people are just naturally bright; me, well I was just . . . natural. Whenever I took an exam in school, I always knew who was going to get up first and hand in their papers, and it was not going to be me. I was the one who was often the last to leave, the teacher drumming her fingers on the desktop hoping I'd get done before dark.

Knowledge is an interesting thing. It seems no matter how much knowledge a person has, it's never enough. Think of the smartest person you've ever met. Chances are good that he or she is not satisfied with how much they know, even though they know more than most people.

The smartest person I know is a friend of mine whom I've known for years. He can talk at length on almost any subject, mainly because he can read up to twenty books a week and remember most of what he's read. He is also an excellent writer, and not only does he have a lot of insight on the subjects about which he writes, but his writing often answers questions that never even occurred to me.

Yet even my good friend doesn't know everything. I can remember one time when I asked him a question and his simple response was, "I don't know." I was shocked. I had begun to think that he knew almost everything. I had so much faith in his opinion on different issues that it was a bit of a letdown to hear him say what he said.

That is something we will never have to worry about with God. The Bible makes it clear that God knows everything—without any kind of limitation or boundary to His knowledge.

In 1 John 3:20, we are told that God "knows all things." A simple statement, yet extremely profound when you start to think about it.

How Much Does God Know?

Can you imagine anyone being bold enough to say that he is all-knowing (which is what the word *omniscient* means)? It takes guts to say such a thing. In fact, the only person who can rightfully make this claim is God, and that's exactly what He does. Take a few moments to read and think about the following verses:

- Job 28:24
- Job 36:4
- Psalm 33:13
- Psalm 38:9
- Isaiah 40:26
- Jeremiah 23:24

God is truly amazing in His knowledge! There is nothing that is possible to know that God does not know. In fact, He is infinite in His knowledge and understanding. That means that those who spend eternity in His presence will never experience an end to their learning about God.

But let's make this very practical. Just what kinds of things does God know?

First, He knows the numbers of hairs on your head (Matthew 10:30). Why would anyone even care how many hairs are on your head? But God knows, just because He knows everything. He doesn't even have to sit there and count them; He just knows because He is God.

Second, He knows how many stars are in the sky. As man does his best to peer into the vast darkness of space with scientific instruments such as the Hubble telescope, God probably yawns at all of our efforts. He knows all about the universe, even the very farthest corners of space that we don't even know exist. He is not at a loss to understand the science involved in planetary rotations, asteroids, solar systems, and galaxies; they are child's play to Him. *He has billions of answers to questions we don't even know enough to ask!*

Third, He knows the day on which you will die (Psalm 139:16). Most people probably don't spend much time thinking about death—and that's OK. But unless Jesus comes back within fifty to one hundred years, all who are reading this book today will experience death—and God knows exactly when, where, and how that will take place.

Tyler came to a Wednesday night youth meeting where he heard a professional football player talk about what it meant to have a relationship with Jesus Christ. Tyler was new to church, and he was impressed with the speaker's words: "For all you know, tonight could be your last night to live, or this could be your last week to live. We just don't know how much time we have left on this earth."

Tyler approached the speaker after the meeting and asked him lots of questions about Christ and what it means to become a child of God. It was only three days later that Tyler was killed in a car accident.

Did Tyler know what was about to happen to him? No, but God knew the exact day, hour, and second when Tyler's life here on earth would end. He knows the same about each one of us.

Fourth, God knows if you will get married, and if so, who it will be and how many kids you will have. Try to picture yourself twenty years from today. Can you do it? Do you know what you will look like, or where you will live, or what your job will be, or what kind of house you will live in? Of course not, not with any degree of accuracy. You may know what you'd like to be doing twenty years from now, but none of us can really know for sure.

Picture yourself in about twenty years as you get ready for your son or daughter's graduation from high school. You sit in the audience as the band plays, and your child walks down the aisle.

He or she looks like you and has many of your traits. You are so proud. Your spouse sits next to you squeezing your hand, both of you a little plumper than you are now; less hair if you're a guy, and more wrinkles if you're a gal. It's kind of hard to imagine, isn't it? But God already knows these things. He knows every detail of your past, present, and future. He is above, and outside of, time and space.

Fifth, He knows if you will continue to walk with Him. Think back for a moment to the story of Judas in the Bible. Judas was one of the twelve closest followers of Jesus when He was on earth. As a disciple, Judas spent a lot of time at Jesus' side, listening to Him teach, watching Him do miracles, and basically learning about God by watching Him in action.

Yet all the time Judas was with Christ, I doubt that Judas knew that someday he would be the one to betray Christ to the authorities so that He would be killed. Yet Jesus knew that Judas was going to betray Him. At their last supper together, when Jesus was giving final instructions to His disciples, He knew that when Judas slipped out into the darkness of night, he was leaving in order to betray Him. Nonetheless, He loved him anyway. (Read John 13.)

My sincere prayer is that everyone who reads this book will never fall away from Christ but will be faithful and fruitful throughout life. Yet even if you were to fall away from Christ for a time, God knows exactly how it will happen and what it will take to bring you back into fellowship with Him.

Sixth, God knows every person who has lived throughout human history, including the names of every person alive today. Do you know the name of your great-great-great-grandfather? Chances are, you don't. Yet even if you do know his name, there's no way you can know him intimately—the way he laughed, the experiences he had in life, the dreams he had for his family, even his particular hopes and fears.

Today, after several generations, there is no one alive who knew your great-great-great-grandfather personally. In fact, probably little or nothing is even remembered about him. Yet God remembers him, just as He knows every single one of the billions of individuals who have lived on this earth since His creation of Adam and Eve.

Seventh, God knows every step you are about to take, what words you are about to say, and the thoughts that go through your head every moment of every day. Read Psalm 139:1–4; it tells just how much God knows about you and me.

Now look up Hebrews 4:13. There are no secrets that can be kept from God. We may be able to fool those around us, but no one can ever keep God from knowing whom we really are deep inside.

Eighth, God knows the day the world will end. With God there are no surprises. His magnificent plan for this world is unfolding exactly as He ordained. All of the events found in the Book of Revelation are happening just as He said they would. There is also a passage there that talks about the time of judgment. (Look up Revelation 11:18.)

What If God Did Not Know Everything There Is to Know?

- The universe would be subject to chaos. Only a supernatural intelligence can keep the planets from colliding, the earth rotating on a proper axis, and our world the proper distance from the sun.
- He could only claim to be a powerful being, with no authority to claim that He alone is God. If He were not all-knowing, He would have no way of knowing whether or not another God exists.
- He could never promise us eternal life, for He would have no way of knowing whether or not He could sustain His people for eternity.
- He would not have been able to predict the coming of the Messiah in the writings of the Old Testament.
- He could never really know us fully because He could only learn about us through observation.

Yet God is a wonderful Father precisely because He knows us so well. He knows every need that we have and exactly how to meet our needs in the best way possible.

Benefits of Belonging to a God Who Knows Everything

- We can trust everything God says about Himself.
- We can trust that when we pray, God is already aware of what we're talking to Him about.
- We can be secure in our salvation. Look up John 10:28–29; it tells us something very comforting. Only a God who is all-knowing could make such a statement. A god who is constantly learning, growing, and developing could never give this kind of eternal assurance.

In Job 37:16 we are told that the God of the Bible is "perfect in knowledge." This is the God who loves you perfectly, pursues your friendship diligently, and knows you completely.

Small Group Discussion

1. Why is it significant that God cannot learn?

2. Since there are no secrets from God, why do we sometimes pretend that He doesn't know our thoughts?

God Is Omnipotent

By all accounts Rick was a pretty cocky young man. He was good looking, had a nice car, and was the subject of girls' glances and whispers whenever he would walk by. To a lot of people, Rick seemed to have it all.

Yes, Rick had the world by the tail; unfortunately, the world had hold of Rick's heart. He was full of himself, and he knew it full well. The problem was, he liked the arrogant feeling of trusting in himself rather than in God. He was content to leave God on the periphery of his life.

When the annual beach retreat came around one year, circumstances forced Rick to drive down late to the coast by himself. He enjoyed hearing the roar of his car's engine as he sped through the coastal range, racing around corners while he daydreamed about the new girls he would meet once he arrived. In his heart he knew he wasn't going to the retreat to hear the Word of God. This was merely an excuse to meet pretty girls—nothing more.

Suddenly Rick's mind was jerked back to reality by the sight of a car pulling out in front of him. He hit the brakes instinctively, sending the tail of his car into a sideways slide. Rick tried to steer out of it, but he overcorrected and flew off the side of the road. As the car hit the bank, it flipped a full turn in the air before landing upside down in the ditch. To Rick, the event seemed to happen in slow motion—papers, clothes, and CDs floating in the air until the car landed on its top.

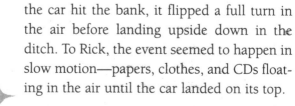

CHAPTER 8

The car was still rocking a bit as Rick, upside down, unhooked his seat belt and slid out the shattered driver's-side window. He stumbled halfway up the steep bank toward the road before he looked back at the crumpled vehicle. All four tires were spinning in the air while oil, gas, and antifreeze formed small pools under the car as they seeped from the engine compartment.

Rick turned his attention to himself. Though he expected to find blood rushing from numerous gashes, there was no blood to be seen. He ran his hands over his face, arms, and legs before he fully realized that he didn't have a single scratch anywhere on his body.

It was then that Rick did something that clearly revealed the arrogance in his heart. Instead of thanking God that he was still alive, let alone unhurt, he lifted both his fists toward the sky and yelled, "See, God, even You can't get me."

Amazingly, this 145-pound young man was shaking his fist in the face of the God of the universe. Rick really believed that he was invincible, that not even God could bring him down.

Rick eventually made it to the retreat. Though he heard the messages and mumbled through some worship songs, his heart remained hard. His mind was on the girls, not on the Father.

How Powerful Is God?

When you think of God, what do you think of? The answer to this question is very important because a wrong view of God is almost always the root cause of wrong thinking and wrong living.

Do you believe that God is powerful? If so, you are in line with what the Bible says about Him. (Look up Jeremiah 32:17.) Think about some of the ways in which God is all-powerful.

God Can Create Something out of Nothing

Imagine how difficult it would be to build a house if you didn't have the materials with which to build it. If you wanted wood, you would have to plant a tree, watch it grow, then cut it down once it was tall. To get glass you'd have to mix sand and water, somehow create a fire, and then shape it into windows. The same with steel, plastic, porcelain, linoleum, carpet, and every other kind of material that goes into building a structure. God, however, didn't begin with any materials at all, not even a seed to plant in order to grow trees.

This is just a glimpse of what God did when He spoke the world into existence. He created the very building blocks of matter, as well as life itself. That takes an incredible amount of power.

God Created the Universe

Scientists are continually amazed at the intricate complexity revealed in the universe around us. The more they dig in the ground, gaze into the sky, and magnify cells with powerful microscopes, the more they see the fingerprints of a powerful designer all over His creation.

God Created Humankind in His Image

Again, the complexity of how our bodies work is purely astounding. Miles and miles of blood vessels wind their way in and between vital organs that all work together to sustain our lives. Yet we are more than physical beings; we are also comprised of mind, emotion, and will.

Basically, it is the sustaining power of God that is allowing you to breathe as you are reading this book. His power sustains you—physically, emotionally, and spiritually—until He knows it's best to call you home. He will then sustain you in His presence forever.

God Is More Powerful than the Mightiest Nations on Earth

Look up Psalm 22:28. Try to imagine how many missiles and warheads there are in the world today. It's been said that humankind has the power to destroy itself many times over. If you've seen pictures of Hiroshima, you know how devastating a nuclear blast can be. Imagine if hundreds or thousands of bombs were to go off at the same time. Now that's incredible power.

Still, God is infinitely more powerful than any weapons humans can invent. In fact, nothing you can ever think of is more powerful than God. Look up 2 Chronicles 20:6.

How God's Power Reassures Us

Remember when you thought your dad was Superman? As a little kid, you would feel his muscles and tug at the hair on his arms. And when the two of you would wrestle on the floor, he would let you win, even though you both knew that he could pin you anytime he wanted. Most kids who have a strong dad in their lives feel secure and safe.

In the same way, we can feel safe and secure in the fact that we have a strong heavenly Father who cares for us. It helps us to know that God is greater than any enemy.

So just what kinds of things reassure us about God's power?

First, it's good to know that God's power is effortless to Him. God doesn't work up a sweat trying to make things happen.

Second, God's power is available to us no matter what kinds of battles we may face. (Look up Psalm 24:7.)

God will give you the power you need to be victorious in every situation. Anthony and his friend often go downtown trying to find people to talk with about Christ. They take blankets and hot chocolate down to the streets and give them out to the homeless. One day they offered some hot chocolate to a guy who was living off a park bench.

"You ——— Christians," said the homeless man. "If you're really such a Christian, why don't you turn your cheek while I hit you?"

Anthony was scared stiff, but he felt that God would take care of him if he turned his cheek. Anthony kept his arms at his side, and, without saying a word, turned the side of his face toward the man. Out of the corner of his eye he saw the man raise his fist as if to strike him, then slowly lower it again.

"OK, what about giving me your sweater? Didn't Jesus say that if someone asks for your sweater, you're supposed to give it to him? I'm asking for your sweater. Give it to me," said the man.

Anthony looked at the man, praying silently that God would help him to do the right thing. "Yeah, Jesus said that, and I'm happy to give it to you in the name of Jesus." With that he pulled the beautiful sweater over his head and gave it to the man. "Here, take it. It's yours."

The man's countenance softened. He was quiet for a moment, staring at Anthony as if he'd just seen a ghost.

"I've never met a Christian like you before," said the homeless man. "You have a lot of faith in your God, don't you?" he said respectfully as he walked away.

Anthony was glad that he had trusted in the power of God for how to respond in this unique situation. He knew that it probably wouldn't be wise to give his clothes to every person who asks, but in this situation he felt that God was prompting him to do just that. He was learning to trust God for everything he needed, even in the midst of such a strange encounter.

The battles you face will probably be different from the one Anthony experienced on that wintry day downtown. Battles come in various shapes and sizes and intensities, but they all have one thing in common: they are winnable when we allow God to exercise His power through us. (Look up Ephesians 3:20–21.)

Third, it's comforting to know that God is powerful enough to keep your soul in His care. (Look up John 10:26–28.)

It's important for you to understand that if you have truly been born again by accepting Christ into your heart and have sincerely asked Him for forgiveness of your sins, then you are His forever. No one can snatch you from His hands.

Look up 1 John 5:11–13; it gives us the assurance that if we have Jesus living in us, then we have eternal life.

The truth is, no one will ever be able to separate you from God's love. That's how powerful His love and care are for you.

Lastly, it's comforting to know that God has the power to change people from the inside out.

One such story comes out of Cambodia, where a mass murderer who ran a torture camp has reportedly given his life to Christ within the last few years. The Khmer Rouge was in power during the 1970s and is responsible for the genocide of more than a million Cambodians during their reign of terror. The man, who is known as Duch, was the director of a Khmer Rouge prison camp from 1974 to 1979, where he personally tortured and killed thousands of people.

A Cambodian pastor from Los Angeles tells of Duch's conversion to Christ. Weighed down by guilt over his past, Duch attended a Christian class where he heard of Christ's forgiveness. At first he was hesitant to believe that even he could be forgiven, but eventually he received the Word with joy and was baptized after making a confession of faith in Christ. He then started a church in his own village before being arrested by Cambodian authorities, who are preparing charges against him.

Can God really forgive someone who has done such horrible evil? Yes, all because of the incredible power of the cross. God can do what to us seems impossible. As you get to know God better and better through His Word, you will find that it becomes easier to trust God and to rest in His amazing power.

Allow God to reveal His power through your life. He is just waiting for you to ask.

Small Group Discussion

1. In what way can pride affect your view of God's power?

2. If God were not omnipotent, how would it affect your relationship with Him? How would it affect your courage when doing what He's called you to do?

God Is Love

Laura and her brother, Tom, stumbled down the living room stairs, stepping over carefully wrapped presents before plopping down on the living room sofa. Still in their robes and rubbing the sleep from their eyes, they didn't notice how excited Mom and Dad were that this morning had finally arrived.

To Laura, it seemed like only a month had gone by since last year's Christmas morning. So much had happened during the previous twelve months, the most important being that she had accepted Christ into her heart during that time. And what a change He had made in her life! She was expecting her most meaningful Christmas Day ever, especially if her family could keep from arguing, which seemed to be an annual Christmas tradition around her house.

Laura's mom was bubbly with excitement. She was especially anxious to see Tom open his present. Her son was getting more difficult to please in his teenage years, and she had shopped long and hard to find him just the right gift. In fact, his gift had been the most difficult to pick out. She'd spent many a late night second-guessing herself as to whether she had bought him something he would really like. Finally, she was confident that she had found him the perfect present.

Laura went first, opening a gift with her name on the tag; it was a sweater. She held it up for everyone to see before bounding over to Mom and Dad to hug them. She was learning to be genuinely grateful for her parents' generosity, something she had long taken for granted.

CHAPTER 9 _____

At Mom's urging, Tom grabbed the biggest present under the tree, and in a nonchalant manner he tore the colorful paper off the box. It was a stereo—an expensive stereo.

Mom looked intently at Tom's face, hoping for the smile that would reassure her that he was pleased. Tom flipped the box over to find the stereo's model number, then looked up with disgust. "This isn't the one I wanted," he snorted.

Mom was crushed; then Dad confronted his son. Tom got up without a word and went up the stairs to his bedroom, leaving the stereo behind and staying in his room for hours. Laura went ahead and opened the rest of her presents with appreciation, but it wasn't the same without Tom. Her parents were deeply wounded by their son's lack of appreciation. It was another blow-up Christmas at Laura's house.

Tom's selfish attitude is shocking to read about, especially in light of his mom's great desire to please him. Yet when was the last time you thanked God for the way He's shown His love to you? Just like Tom, a selfish heart has difficulty recognizing the Father's incredible giving nature.

If people don't know the Father personally, they cannot recognize the love of God and His incredible goodness. They are blinded by sin—driven by pure selfishness. Yet God still provides for them in countless ways: the affection of family and friends, a job by which to support loved ones, the sun and rain causing crops to grow. All of these things, and many more, are evidence of God's incredible goodness to both those who know Him and those who choose to ignore Him.

Jesus experienced this kind of rejection on many occasions. There are numerous examples in the Bible of those who chose to reject Jesus and His gift of grace, but one in particular illustrates the hard heart of humans. (Look up Luke 17:12–19.)

Our first response to this story is, "I would never do that." But the truth is, we are all guilty of being ungrateful toward God. Now that you are a follower of Christ, begin to put on the eyes of thankfulness, like Laura did that Christmas morning. Your Father in heaven is a gift giver. (Look up James 1:17.)

God's very nature is to be generous, and this generosity is born out of His love. The Bible tells us that "God is love" (1 John 4:16).

Imagine that you decided to purchase a fifty-dollar gift for your best friend because of your commitment and love for him or her. If your friend were to open it and say nothing—no response, no thank you, nothing—how would that make you feel? As insulting as that would be, so it is with us when we lack appreciation for the love and goodness of God.

So, just what has God done for you? Here are a few things to consider.

First, God has provided you with daily provisions. For instance, think about where your food comes from. Most of us have it brought to the kitchen table by our mom and/or dad; they've kept the refrigerator stocked for as long as we can remember. Yet who provides the money to buy the food? And who provides the work in order to earn the money? Beyond that, who provides the sun, rain, and seed that make the food possible?

Of course you know the answer (and it's not the federal government!). God is the one who ultimately keeps you fed, and He does so because He loves you.

Amazingly, His love never ceases or fades away. Have you ever known individuals who are hard to love? It kind of wears you out just being around them, doesn't it? Yet God never gets worn out in loving you. He takes pleasure in loving you, no matter who you are or what you've done. (Look up Psalm 36:5.)

Perhaps the clearest expression of God's love is the cross of Jesus Christ. The sacrifice He made on our behalf is greater than we can ever imagine, yet He would have died for you if you were the only person on earth. (Look up Galatians 2:20.)

That, my friend, is true love. But it goes even deeper, for Christ didn't die for us because we are such good people. On the contrary, in our natural state we are enemies of God (Romans 5:10). You see, God even loves those who hate His guts. We all know people who use Jesus' name as a swear word whenever they can. They seem to be totally ignorant of anything God has done for them and are bitter at Him for the fact that He even exists. Yet in the midst of that kind of bitterness, God sent His Son.

God doesn't just say, "I love you"; His actions back up His words. Every second God is loving you—even at this moment, God is loving you. When you do the stupidest, most embarrassing thing you can think of—God is still loving you.

What Is the Depth of His Love for You?

Look for a moment at Ephesians 2:4–5. Think of a person whom you would die for because your love for him or her is so strong. Chances are, you love this person because he or she loves you back. You enjoy their company, and it feels good to be around them. In other words, your love for them is rewarded by their love in return.

God's love, however, is different from ours. He doesn't love us because of our performance or because we are worthy of His love. No, He loves us because *it is His nature to love us.*

Now think for a minute about a scenario that I hope will never happen. Imagine that you are in a serious automobile accident and you survive, but for the rest of your life you remain disfigured and bedridden. Name the person or persons whom you believe would remain by your side. Those who stick by you would be exhibiting an incredible love, wouldn't they? Yet this is but a shadow of God's love for you.

Why Some People Have a Hard Time Accepting God's Love

Some people have experienced such tragic pain in life that it's difficult for them to accept God's gracious love. An example of this is a young man named Larry, who grew up in an emotionally unhealthy home.

Larry's dad was on drugs and wasn't home much. His mother had numerous boyfriends, one of whom would go out of his way to say "I hate you" to Larry on a regular basis.

At a New Year's party, the boyfriend got drunk and pulled out a butcher knife. He grabbed Larry, who was six years of age, and held the knife to the young boy's throat. "I'm going to slit your throat wide open," he said with a wicked smile. Larry didn't know if he was serious or just kidding around, but his mom saw what was happening and flew across the room. In a fit of rage, she grabbed the knife and started stabbing her boyfriend. He died right in front of the young boy's eyes.

Within a few days, Larry and his sister were in foster care. His mom was sent to prison for many years. Larry's sister has since prayed to receive Christ, but Larry is yet to draw close to His heavenly Father. He has trouble believing that a loving God would allow him to grow up the way he did.

What Larry doesn't understand is that God was with him during every moment of his life. We don't know why God allows horrible things to happen, but we do know that God Himself is not immune to pain and suffering. He watched His Son die on a crude Roman torture tool, choosing to stand aside so that greater purposes could be achieved. Somehow, in some way, Larry, too, will see God's great purposes achieved if He submits his will to the will of his Creator.

A second reason why some people will not receive the love of God is because sin is out of control in their lives. They feel unworthy to receive God's forgiveness; therefore, they tend to reject His love.

What the Love of God Will Do

- The love of God brings eternal security. (Look up Romans 8:39.)
- God's love also gives us emotional security. (Look up Matthew 11:28–30.) Sin will take its toll on our emotions and our consciences. Jesus, however, tells us to come to Him, and we will experience peace and rest for our souls.
- The love of God will also bring us to repentance for our sins. (Look up Romans 2:4.) It is God's love that brings us to repentance, not His punishment. The infinite love of God is showered down on those of us who have come to a personal relationship with Him.

Small Group Discussion

1. It's easy for us to expect or demand love from others, yet how can you prevent yourself from taking the love of God for granted?

2. What is the difference between just saying "I love you" to a person versus showing your love in a tangible way? Write out some practical ways in which you experience God's love toward you every day.

God Is a Jealous God

From all outward appearances, Patty seemed to have the perfect husband. Jim was a committed family man, with several wonderful kids and a thriving business. He was a man who knew how to pray and read Scripture, and he did well at raising his children in the ways of God. Jim's commitment level at church was also extraordinary, and he had enjoyed many leadership positions over the years.

Yes, Jim seemed to have it all together—until it all fell apart.

Underneath Jim's calm exterior lay a vulnerability that was surprising to everyone, especially Patty. Maybe even Jim was surprised when he started to take delight in spending time with a new female associate at work, Carla. She was pretty, a committed Christian, and full of fun and energy. When she began to pay him a little too much attention, he scoffed at the warning bells going off in his head.

"She's a sister in Christ; that's all," he would tell himself. "After all, we're both happily married. There's nothing wrong with spending a little time together."

Soon he was going out of his way to spend time with his "friend." He would make up excuses to be with Carla, coming in on days off just to see how she was doing. All the while, his home life was becoming strained. For a number of years he had been sensing a loss of intimacy with Patty. He'd always thought it was due to the seasons of life that all marriages go through, but now he began to wonder.

Perhaps he and Patty had never been right for each other all along. Sure, God had given

CHAPTER 10

them some wonderful kids together, and they enjoyed memories from along the way. But maybe Patty wasn't created to be his soul mate. Maybe his true soul mate was Carla at the office.

At first Jim resisted the idea. After all, he was a family man and a Christian. He couldn't just walk out on his family, could he? Slowly, however, he realized that he had fallen in love with Carla, and it became obvious that she felt the same about him.

Jim came home from work one evening and told Patty he needed to talk to her about something very important. They waited until the kids had left for the evening before sitting down on the living room sofa. Jim calmly explained that he didn't love Patty anymore. In fact, he said he had never really loved her as much as she thought he did. He lied to her by saying that he wasn't involved with anyone else, and then he asked her for a divorce.

While sitting on the living room sofa that evening, Patty's world shattered and fell apart in jagged pieces. She had sensed that their marriage was in trouble, but she figured it was due to the stress of owning their own business. It wasn't until a few days after his announcement that she heard rumors about Jim and Carla. At first Jim denied them as gossip, but finally he admitted the rumors were true. His only regret was that he hadn't found Carla years ago.

You can imagine the range of emotions that Patty felt—anger, sadness, betrayal, and of course, jealousy. Yes, Patty was jealous—and rightly so. Someone took something precious that rightfully belonged to her—her home, her marriage, her husband. She was angry, she was hurt, and she was rightfully jealous.

God Is a Jealous God

It's common to think of jealousy only as a negative trait. That's because it is usually used in a derogatory sense, such as "Aw, you're just jealous," or "Come on, don't be so jealous of him or her." Jealousy, however, can be a godly attribute when applied toward the right objects.

The proof of this is that God is a jealous God—He says so right in the Bible. (Read Exodus 34:14.) But God is never jealous of things; He is only jealous for His people. The only time we see God as jealous in the Bible is when people who belong to Him are foolishly wandering away from Him.

God is jealous for those who rightfully belong to Him, just as you are jealous for those things that rightfully belong to you. For instance, if you become committed to someone in marriage, you will have the right to be jealous of that person; in God's eyes, your spouse belongs to you just as you belong to him or her.

Jealousy, however, is not to be confused with the sin of envy. Envy is a longing for something, or someone, that is not rightfully ours. Since God is the Creator of the universe, He has every right to expect that people should worship and obey Him. When they don't, He experiences jealousy, much as you and I would if a loved one walked out on us.

In Patty's case, if she hadn't experienced jealousy for Jim, it would have meant that she didn't truly love him. In the same way, God's jealousy for people is a result of His deep love for the human race. If He weren't a jealous God, then His commitment to you and me might be called into question.

When Does God Get Jealous?

The Bible tells us of several things that arouse God's jealousy.

First, God is jealous for the sake of His name. (Read Ezekiel 39:25.) In the Old Testament, a name was more than a title by which one differentiated individuals; it was a way of declaring a person's character or position in life.

Sometimes people would experience a change of their name to better reflect who they were. For instance, when we first meet Abraham in the Book of Genesis, he is called Abram, which means "exalted father." Later, God changes Abram's name to Abraham, meaning "father of a multitude." God did this because the latter name reflected that which Abraham was becoming.

God is jealous for His name because it declares who He is. He is concerned that when people speak His name, they do so with respect and a proper sense of fear—something both fitting for the

King of the universe and healthy for those who were created by Him.

As believers, we are to do everything "to the glory of God" (1 Corinthians 10:31). Since we now belong to Him, we are to live for Him and not for ourselves.

God says in Isaiah 48:11, "My glory I will not give another." This isn't because God is conceited; it's because He is the one Person in the universe who is worthy of all glory. To not give glory to Him is to rebel against Him as Creator.

Second, God is jealous for His people. He is a God of love, but He is also an avenging God, jealous for His children. In the Old Testament Book of Nahum, we read these powerful words:

> A jealous and avenging God is the LORD;
> The LORD is avenging and wrathful.
> The LORD takes vengeance on His adversaries,
> And He reserves wrath for His enemies. (Nahum 1:2)

Before you think that God is an angry dictator, however, look at the very next verse:

> The LORD is slow to anger and great in power,
> And the LORD will by no means leave the guilty
> unpunished. (Nahum 1:3)

Our heavenly Father is the perfect combination of love and justice. He is full of love and slow to anger, yet He will not—and cannot—resist justice by not punishing evil. The evil that we experience in this world arouses God's holy jealousy. One day He will make all things right by judging those who resist His rightfully jealous claim to their lives.

A student named Eric was walking across the courtyard at school one morning when he saw two male homosexual students kissing each other in plain view. As ridiculous as this was, Eric was even more upset by the fact that a teacher was also present in the courtyard, doing nothing to stop the two young men.

Eric, being a journalism student, decided to write an editorial for the school newspaper. In the article he chastised the two students for their lack of dignity and morals but also confronted the faculty for not being more rigid in enforcing the school rules.

The reaction Eric received was surprising. A number of the teachers became openly upset with him for writing the article, while many more liberal students taunted Eric for being such a "prude" and a "goody-two-shoes."

Eric, in writing the article, was being jealous for decency and morality at his school. He was not willing to stand aside and let evil take over without a fight. In the same way, God is jealous for His name and for His people. One day, when sin has run its course, He will make all things right. He will judge sin and reward righteousness, though we may not see it now.

Third, God becomes jealous when one of His children turns his or her back and falls in love with the world. God wants our affections to be for Him and for the things that please Him, not for the things of the world. Read James 4:4–5; it contains a strong warning for those who are prone to turn their backs on God.

Todd is a young man who came to Christ during his high school years. He lived a zealous life for the Lord and was outspoken on campus about his faith. He enjoyed the cleanness and openness that he was experiencing with the Lord, having previously lived a lifestyle of drug and alcohol abuse.

Todd began to change, however, when he graduated from high school. It started when he began to go to his old drug buddies in order to share Christ with them. The more he talked to them, the more attractive his old lifestyle began to appear. After awhile, Todd began to lose His love for the Father and to fall in love with the world all over again.

Within a short amount of time, Todd had fallen hard. He began smoking pot and chasing girls, just like he did before he came to Christ. His heart grew cold, and he began to get deeper into drugs and to become sexually active. What it says in 2 Peter 2:22 became true of Todd: "It has happened to them according to the true proverb, 'A dog returns to its own vomit,' and, 'A sow, after washing, returns to wallowing in the mire.'"

In time, Todd felt so guilty that he knew he couldn't continue in sin. He thought the sin would bring him pleasure, but instead it brought him misery. He had tasted what it was like to walk with God in purity, and he began to long for Christ once again.

Eventually Todd repented of his sin and came back to the Lord. What Todd didn't realize at the time was that he was experiencing the jealousy of God; God was putting pressure on Todd's heart so that he would return and repent of his sin. God's jealousy was evidence of this great love and forgiveness.

God is jealous for your affections. He wants you to desire Him more than any other thing in this world. Be thankful for His jealous nature. It is proof of His undying love for you. Don't be jealous of those who are living for worldly pleasures. Respond to God by being jealous for His glory. Seek to honor Him every day, in every circumstance, with all your strength.

You'll be eternally thankful that you did.

Small Group Discussion

1. Think of a time when you experienced the jealousy of God in your own life. What are some of the poor choices you made that then caused God to pull you back to Himself?

2. Is it ever right for a believer to be jealous? Explain your answer.

God Is All-Wise

Todd's dad was clear in his instructions, his smile doing little to cover the seriousness of his words.

"Son, I'm going to let you drive the tractor this evening on one condition—that you keep it slow, and I mean very slow. We don't want anyone getting hurt."

A quick nod and a grin meant that Todd understood, and then the boy was off to start preparing for the Halloween party to be held that evening. Todd and his dad had hay bales to place and decorations yet to hang in the old barn, and time was not standing still. Soon the youth group would arrive and the party would begin.

A harvest moon rose full and bright over the farm as kids began arriving later that evening. Soon the party was in full swing, and when Todd jumped on the old tractor and turned the key, blue smoke and a loud purr from the exhaust pipe let everyone know it was time for a hayride.

Todd felt a rush of importance as the kids ran from the barn, jumping wildly onto the trailer that was hitched to the old John Deere. When everyone was aboard, Todd slipped the giant lever into low gear and gently released the clutch. With a lurch, the tractor tugged the screaming kids into motion as they headed out for a turn around the field.

At first the kids were satisfied with the tractor's slow speed, but gradually they began to yell, "Faster, Todd . . . faster, Todd." Todd turned and smiled, shrugging his shoulders as if to say, "Sorry guys, this is top speed for tonight."

CHAPTER 11

"Come on, Todd, can't you speed this thing up a little?" yelled some of his friends. Todd pulled the throttle back an inch, giving a bit more power but barely going any faster than before.

Todd could hear his father's voice in his head as he flirted with the temptation of popping the old tractor into a higher, and faster, gear. He knew that he would be directly disobeying his dad, but maybe his dad wouldn't notice since he was still back at the barn. The kids' cries grew louder, and as they did, his father's voice seemed to decrease in importance. *After all,* he reasoned to himself, *I want to show my friends a good time.*

It took Todd several minutes to make the decision but only a split second to act on it. Instead of shifting gears, he decided to make a quick turn down a steep hill in order to gain speed. The kids screamed with excitement as the tractor and trailer turned from its predictable course and headed downhill. Todd gripped the steering wheel tightly; he wasn't used to the weight of the loaded trailer behind him, which threatened to push him off the road and onto a steep bank.

Todd throttled back and pushed on the brake, but the weight behind him was pushing too hard. Panic gripped him as the tractor veered out of control. The youth pastor, who was riding on the trailer, saw what was happening and began throwing students off the back. By the time the last student jumped off, Todd was completely at the mercy of the raging machine. The tractor roared off the path, hit the steep bank, and flipped onto its back, crushing Todd under its massive weight.

Giant wheels were spinning in the air as Todd's panicked father arrived breathlessly at the tragic scene. He had started running the moment he saw Todd go for the hill, knowing that only an experienced driver could maneuver the steep grade safely. Now his worst fears were realized as he watched the life drain out of his son's body.

He grabbed Todd and pulled with all his might, but the weight of the giant machine lay fully on the boy, crushing him mercilessly. It was obvious that there was no escape.

"If you'd only listened to me, son" were the only words the father could utter. "Why didn't you listen to what I said? Why didn't you listen!" he cried as he held his boy in his arms, every father's nightmare coming true before his very eyes.

What a tragic story, for many reasons. First, because a precious life was lost and an entire family now experiences incredible pain. And second, because it was such a senseless act, a split-second decision resulting in a horribly tragic accident. Todd ignored the wise counsel of his father and paid the ultimate price.

Why Seek God's Wisdom?

The above story illustrates a very important aspect of the Christian life: when we listen to God's wisdom and obey it, we will be blessed; when we ignore God's wisdom, it brings painful consequences to our lives and to the lives of those around us.

The Bible talks a lot about wisdom and foolishness. It makes it clear that wisdom comes from God. (Read Proverbs 3:7.)

Sometimes it helps to compare our limited wisdom with God's infinite wisdom. For instance:

- Do you know every complex detail of all that happened before you arrived in the world? No.
- Did you create yourself, in all the complexity of your social, physical, spiritual, and emotional elements? No.
- Do you have a complete understanding of how the universe operates? No.

We don't know these things, but God does! Think about that fact for a minute. He knows everything there is to know. If God were in your chemistry class, He would never need to study—He created chemistry, geometry, algebra, and every other subject you'll ever study in school.

Yet more important than knowing facts and figures, God knows how life works. He understands the beauty of love and the power of friendship. He also comprehends the destructive power of sin, and that is why He offers us His wisdom. It's free to all who will receive it.

How to Find Wisdom

As you read this chapter, it should stimulate within you a growing desire to live life according to God's wisdom. If so, that's awesome! But where do you go from here? How does a person acquire wisdom—this incredible gift that the Bible says is more precious than gold or silver? Here are several ways.

First, seek to know God by knowing His precious Word, the Bible. In Psalms and Proverbs, we are told over and over again that "the fear of the LORD is the beginning of wisdom" (Psalm 111:10). The word *fear* in this context means "to revere, honor, and respect." This is the starting place for those who seek to be wise.

Don't ever think that you can ignore the Bible and still live a life that is pleasing to God. It's impossible. Do the best you can to read God's Word on a daily basis. If you ignore it, you are ignoring pure gold!

Second, ask God to give you wisdom. (Read James 1:5.) Don't hesitate to ask God for directions if you don't know what to do in a given situation. He will show you His will for your life if you patiently wait on Him.

Third, find ways to hang out with people who walk with God. Let their lives be a model for how you should live. Seek counsel from more mature believers; you'll find that God often speaks through them as you seek to know God's will.

John was a brand-new Christian when he started meeting with his pastor on a regular basis. He was full of questions concerning many areas of his new walk with Christ, but one area in particular caused him a lot of concern: sex.

John was old enough to be living away from his parents, and he planned to move in with his girlfriend in order to save money. Besides, he thought it would be a good way to see if they were compatible enough to get married someday. Because John had been raised in a non-Christian home, he didn't see sex as something that needed to be saved until marriage.

As John and his pastor studied the Bible together, John began to see God's wisdom on this subject. He began to understand why

God wanted sex to be sacred between a husband and wife and how sex outside of marriage was harmful in so many ways.

John's views on sex radically changed. Whereas John once believed that living with a girl before marriage made total sense, he soon learned that in God's eyes it is total foolishness. Now, as John looks back on that season of life, he knows that God's wisdom spared him from an incredible amount of pain and regret—and guilt. He eventually broke up with his girlfriend and spent two years getting to know God. Because John listened to the wisdom and counsel of mature believers, he is now in a relationship that is Christ centered.

God's wisdom acts as a guardrail that keeps us from falling off the cliff of our own foolish desires.

What Wisdom Produces

Tom and Bill were best friends while growing up. Both of them were raised in good homes, with the kind of parents who attended every sporting event in which their kids were involved. The boys shared many of the same opportunities to learn about God at church and youth group. Both were outstanding students, and both played on a basketball team that went to the state playoffs. Since high school, however, their lives have turned out very differently. Tom lives on the streets, his eyes constantly looking for a quick fix for happiness. He has squandered his life on drugs, alcohol, and sex—all of which have left him empty and dissatisfied with life. Still, he chases the wisdom of the world, believing the lie that his ways are better than the wise ways of God.

Bill, on the other hand, has followed the path that his parents taught him. He finished college and married a wonderful girl. They have a great marriage, a loving child, and a happiness that is deep and enduring.

Two young men, two paths—two differing results. It's just like in the Old Testament Book of Proverbs where wisdom and foolishness are personified as two ladies who are trying to get one's attention. Proverbs 9:3–6 (NKJV) tells us first of Lady Wisdom's cry:

She cries out from the highest places of the city,
"Whoever is simple, let him turn in here!"
As for him who lacks understanding, she says to him,
"Come, eat of my bread
And drink of the wine I have mixed.
Forsake foolishness and live,
And go in the way of understanding."

She continues in verses 10–11:
"The fear of the LORD is the beginning of wisdom,
And the knowledge of the Holy One is understanding.
For by me your days will be multiplied,
And years of life will be added to you."

Lady Foolishness, however, is "clamorous."
She is simple, and knows nothing."
For she sits at the door of her house,
On a seat by the highest places of the city,
To call to those who pass by,
Who go straight on their way:
"Whoever is simple, let him turn in here";
And as for him who lacks understanding, she says to him,
"Stolen water is sweet,
And bread eaten in secret is pleasant."
But he does not know that the dead are there,
That her guests are in the depths of hell.
(Proverbs 9:13–18)

What an amazing picture: two ladies calling out for attention and two paths from which to choose. One leads to supernatural understanding and a blessed life; the other path leads to emptiness in this life, and its guests "are in the depths of hell."

This is poetic language, often used in the Old Testament to make truth come alive in the reader's imagination. It's not telling us that anyone who makes an occasional foolish choice, or even many foolish choices, is automatically going to hell. If you have invited Christ into your heart and have asked Him to forgive you for your sin, then He has promised that you will be with Him in heaven. Period.

The point of the story is what you and I are faced with every day, and that is the issue of choices. If you follow Lady Wisdom (the fear of the Lord), your life will be blessed in wonderful ways. If you follow Lady Foolishness (doing things your own way), you will experience brokenness and pain in this life.

So what kinds of choices are we talking about? Basic things, such as:

- the friends you choose
- the music you listen to
- the movies or TV you watch
- the attitude you show toward your parents and those in authority
- the frequency with which you attend church and a student ministry
- the clothes you wear
- the language you use
- the magazines you read
- the thoughts you allow to dwell in your mind

Carrie was somewhat of an ugly duckling in junior high. She was underdeveloped and skinny as a rail; few boys even knew that she was alive. But all that changed when she got to high school. Her body began to change, and before long she caught up with her peers and even surpassed them.

Carrie had the looks that all the girls envied and all the boys desired. She began to play on that, choosing clothes that accentuated her developing body. The more attention she received, the tighter her clothes became. Without really understanding what was happening, she became addicted to turning guys on through her seductive dress.

If Carrie had stopped to consider God's wisdom on this issue, she would have changed her behavior and her clothes. But she craved the attention, even though it promised her nothing but heartache and a ruined reputation.

These days Carrie has the "used" look about her; she gave away her innocence at a very high cost. It could have been easily avoided if she had stopped to consider the counsel of God.

Simple everyday choices determine the kind of person you will become: wise or foolish.

The choice is yours.

Small Group Discussion

1. Have you ever ignored the counsel of God? How has this brought great pain to you and to your family?

2. List three action steps you can take to grow in the wisdom of God.

God Is the Trinity

Have you ever felt lonely?

Loneliness is a part of being human. We feel it when a good friend moves far away or when a loving grandparent dies. It happens when parents get divorced and one moves out of the house. It can even happen when a dog or cat you grew up with has to be buried in the backyard.

Loneliness hurts. And though we don't like to think about it, each of us knows what it feels like to be alone, hoping for a relationship that will fill the void deep inside us.

Sheryl experienced the deepest level of loneliness on a daily basis. She was a young high school student who tried her best to fit in but was never able to break through the glass walls that seemed to surround her social life.

Sheryl didn't have any friends—not even one. Her parents loved her, and she never doubted their commitment. But she desperately wanted a friend, any friend—someone to hang out with or to call on the phone. Someone to sit with at lunch, or maybe go see a movie with on Saturday afternoons. But there were no friends. Her phone never rang, and her Saturday afternoons were spent alone in her room at home. Day after day at school, she sat for lunch in the same seat at the same table in the same way—alone.

Sheryl's story is tragic. It's tragic because somehow each of us knows, deep down in our gut, that people are made for relationships. And when we see someone like Sheryl, someone who is nobody's friend, we pity her—and breathe a sigh of relief that we're not in the same situation.

CHAPTER 12

Alone. The very word can make us edgy and uncomfortable. Yet sometimes when we think of God, we think that He, too, must be all alone, that He has no one to relate to or identify with. After all, there's no one else like God in the entire universe. Certainly you and I aren't like Him. The angels are created beings too. Does God ever feel lonely?

Imagine being stranded on a deserted island for the rest of your life—just you, all by yourself. There's no TV, no radio, and no computer—no means by which to contact the outside world. After awhile you would get lonely—really lonely! Sure, there would be animals to talk to, as well as palm trees, crabs, and even bananas. (Just be careful when they start talking back!) But lack of human companionship would probably drive you crazy after being there for many years.

Is that how God feels in this universe? All alone, with no other person to fill the void of His loneliness?

No, God is not lonely. He does not *need* our companionship or our obedience to feel complete within Himself. He doesn't measure His self-esteem based on whether or not we like Him or need Him. God is complete within Himself. All of His relational needs are met within the fact of His very essence—the Trinity.

What Is the Trinity?

There is no question that the God of the Bible is one God. Christians are not polytheists—those who believe in many gods. (Look up Deuteronomy 6:4.)

Don't ever let anyone convince you that the Bible teaches there is more than one God. That's just not true. (Look up Isaiah 42:8 and James 2:19.)

What confuses some people is that this one God who has revealed Himself in the Bible actually consists of three separate persons: Father, Son, and Holy Spirit. It's been said that these three persons of the Trinity are "distinct in personality, yet one in essence." Yes, difficult to understand, yet true nonetheless.

Perhaps someone has told you that the Trinity is not an accurate way of viewing God; they may point to the fact that the word

Trinity can't be found anywhere in the Bible. That's true; the word is not found. However, the truth of the concept is discussed throughout the Bible's pages, from Genesis to Revelation. Here are some things the Bible teaches us about the Trinity:

- The Father, the Son, and Holy Spirit all share the same eternal attributes. They are equal in their deity, which means they are equally God (i.e., there is no "lesser" god and "greater" God). The Bible tells us that all three Persons were present at Creation and all play a significant part in our salvation. They all share those things that make God, God—eternality, omniscience, omnipresence, holiness, etc. (Look up Genesis 1:26.)
- The Father, Son, and Holy Spirit coexist with each other at the same time. It's not as if the Father "morphs" into the Son sometimes, who then changes into the Spirit when needed. (Look up Matthew 3:16–17.)
- The Father, Son, and Holy Spirit are equal in essence but distinct in their roles. For instance, the Son has subjected Himself to the will of the Father. This does not mean that He is less than the Father, but only that He is pleased to submit Himself to the Father's will. Look up John 3:16; notice who did the giving. And again in 2 Corinthians 1:21–22 we see that God (the Father) gave us both Jesus and the Holy Spirit.

As we read the Scriptures carefully, we begin to understand that there is no dissension within the Trinity; there is no infighting, gossip, or secret desire on the part of one to be greater than the others. They enjoy the only perfect relationship this universe has ever seen, from eternity past until eternity future.

God is one—and God is three. Difficult to grasp? Absolutely. Beyond human reason? Kind of! But is it true? *Definitely!*

You Mean God Doesn't Need Me?

Now we come back to our initial question: Is God ever lonely? No, He never is. As a Triune God, He has complete fellowship within Himself. If God had never created the earth or the stars, or the sun or even you and me, He would still be completely happy and satisfied because He is absolutely complete within Himself.

This means that God is not dependent upon us for His happiness. We exist as a means to bring Him further glory, not to meet an emotional need on His part.

The fact that God is the Trinity and that He exists in a perfect, eternal relationship with Himself should give us courage in our own relationship with Him. When you communicate with the Father, He is not learning about relationships in the process. The only reason you can relate to Him in the first place is because *He is a relational God.*

Can You Understand the Trinity?

Stacey was a young girl who professed to know Christ as her personal Savior. She was involved in Bible studies, proclaiming her faith and actively living out her desire to know God more.

One day she met Mark at a Bible study. He was new to the group and had a lot of questions about the reliability of the Bible. Sometimes the two talked for hours on the phone, and Mark's biggest question seemed to always center around the Trinity: how could God be one, yet also be three? He just couldn't understand how people could believe this to be true.

Stacey tried to explain to Mark that it was a concept taught in the Bible, yet when he asked her to show him where the word *Trinity* was found, she eventually gave up looking. It wasn't there.

As Mark explained his view of God, Stacey found that her growing love for him clouded her ability to see the Scriptures clearly. Mark was a Mormon, and he said that it was only logical that there are many gods and that someday we, too, would become divine. He said that it was shortsighted to think that there is only one God.

As Mark opened his Book of Mormon, he showed Stacey some passages that talked about many gods, passages like Abraham 3:15 and 4:3, 10, 25, that say, "And they (the Gods) said, 'Let there be light,' and there was light," or "And the Gods pronounced the dry land, Earth," or "And the Gods organized the earth to bring forth the beasts after their kind."

Mormons teach something called "the law of progression." They believe that when a person dies, the person can become a god. Each god will have a planet of his or her own, ruling much like Elohim does today.

This is in direct opposition to the Bible's clear teaching: there is no other God than the God of Abraham, Isaac, and Jacob—the God of Israel and the Father of our Lord Jesus Christ. Isaiah 44:6 says, "I am the first and I am the last, and there is no God besides Me." God has always been; no one created Him. *He has never changed, and He never will change* (Hebrews 13:8).

Unfortunately, Stacey did not know her Bible well enough to know that the Book of Mormon, and Mark, are mistaken in their concept of God. Stacey fell for a lie because she did not know the truth.

In the Bible, we are given many reasons to trust in God. Don't let an unanswerable question keep you from enjoying a relationship with Him who is beyond the grasp of our imagination.

God is One.

God is the Trinity.

God is relational.

The fact that He is all three gives us confidence that we, too, can have a meaningful relationship with Him, for He understands intimacy. This is why you sometimes hear the phrase "a personal relationship with God." It means that He wants to relate to you on a personal basis, not like a dictator relates to His subjects.

Small Group Discussion

1. Why did God create you? Was it for the purpose of meeting His emotional needs, or was it for His pleasure? Explain.

2. In your opinion, does the Trinity consist of three separate Gods or of one God who exists in three separate persons? Explain your answer. Why is this important?

3. What is it like to experience loneliness? How is it that we can take our loneliness to God and come away filled with His peace?

PART 3
The Essentials

The Deity of Christ

Jerry sat near the edge of his seat, hunched over a small table with his arms outstretched before him.

"OK, Jerry, now place your fingers lightly on the disk and then ask a question. That's it; don't press too hard."

Jerry's friend, Jim, coached him from across the candlelit table. The room was dark, the candles providing just enough light to make out the Ouija board that stretched between them. This was Jerry's first experience with the occultic "game." Jim had told him that the board could tell one's future. Jerry decided to give it a test.

"When am I going to get married?" he asked, not really sure to whom, or what, he was speaking. The disk started to move under his fingers. He wasn't forcing it; he knew he wasn't—it was moving on it's own.

"Don't press too hard, Jer; just touch it lightly. Look, it's heading for a number!" Jim whispered loudly.

The disk moved from number to number until it had given the message: exactly five years to the day from that very evening.

"Wow, Jim—let me ask it something else. This is cool." Jerry ignored the red flag he sensed in his spirit. He had been warned at church that he should never play with Ouija boards, but this was too cool! Besides, church was getting a little too stuffy for him lately. He wanted to branch out and experience some of what the world had to offer.

Jerry had gone to church for most of his young life. Now, as a mid-teenager, he was having a hard time believing in the truth that Jesus was real. When he met Jim at

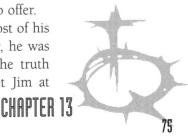

CHAPTER 13

school, Jerry knew he'd found a person who could introduce him to another way of life, an avenue that Jerry was ready to explore.

Jim had never set foot in a church. In fact, he would curse and swear anytime Jerry mentioned God, the Bible, and especially the name of Jesus. It wasn't long 'til Jim had introduced Jerry to drugs and raspy heavy-metal music. Now Jerry was learning about the occult as well.

Over the next several months Jerry got more and more involved with the Ouija board. He was fascinated at how accurate it could be when answering questions, and every so often he and Jim would call out the names of demons as they asked for hidden knowledge. Jerry became fascinated with witchcraft and black magic, and this combined with the drugs and heavy-metal music gave him a sense of self-importance and control that he'd never felt before.

During these months Jerry stopped going to church altogether. His parents pleaded with him to come back, but he had no interest. He'd found a new source of power. He didn't need Jesus in his life anymore—or so he thought.

One Sunday evening his parents laid down an ultimatum: either Jerry was to begin attending church again, or he would have to find another place to live. It was a harsh rule, and Jerry yelled, slammed doors, and threatened to move out. But eventually common sense got the better of him. He realized he had no other means of eating three meals a day.

So that evening Jerry was in church with his parents, sitting in a pew for the first time in months. He did everything he could to ignore the service, but when the pastor started to preach about Jesus and His blood shed on the cross, Jerry became extremely uncomfortable. He started to sweat, and he felt a panicky feeling he'd never felt before.

A dark voice whispered to his mind, *Get out of here; get out of here now.*

Jerry looked for an easy escape, but there was none; he was sitting in the middle of the row. As the pastor's message got stronger, the dark voice also increased in intensity. Soon Jerry's mind was bombarded by profanity and murderous thoughts.

Jerry felt out of control—like he was going crazy. The room began spinning, and by the time everyone stood to sing a final hymn, he was scared that something horrible was happening to him.

Jerry's parents saw the wild and confused look in their son's eyes. It was a look of fear and panic that let them know something serious was happening inside their son.

After the service, Jerry found himself in the pastor's office, his parents and the pastor listening with concern as he shared his recent fascination with the occult.

"I never meant for it to go this far," he said through tears. "I feel like I've given a part of my soul to someone or something else, and now it's scaring me."

The pastor opened his Bible and then looked the boy squarely in the eyes. "Jerry, I'm going to read some Scriptures and then pray for you and ask Jesus to release you from the bondage that you're in right now. I want you to know that Jesus can set you free, and that there's no power that can stand before the name of Jesus."

As the pastor read the verses about Jesus' power, Jerry felt a voice well up inside him. It wasn't his voice—it was the voice of someone dark and evil, more of a growl than anything else.

"You don't own this boy, I do!" screamed the voice through Jerry's mouth. "Leave us alone. I have nothing to do with you."

The pastor looked at Jerry, speaking toward him but not to him. "Demon, you have no authority in this place. Listen to the Scriptures and what they say." He started to read from Ephesians 1:19–23. The pastor spoke again toward Jerry. "It's not in my name, evil spirit, but in the name of Jesus that I command you to flee."

The demon began to curse at the pastor, filthy words rolling out of Jerry's mouth. But the pastor held his ground, and Jerry's parents held on to their boy, praying with all their might. Eventually the victory was realized in Jerry's life that evening; after a long and intense spiritual battle, the demon was forced to leave. Everyone in the room was exhausted, but smiles and hugs and prayers of thanksgiving filled the room before they left the church that night.

And most important of all, Jerry gave his life to Christ that evening. His involvement with Jim and the things of darkness were over. He was now a new person in Jesus Christ.

The Powerful Name of Jesus

There is something very powerful about the name of Jesus. That's why the pastor didn't try to get the demon to leave in his own name, or in Muhammad's name, or in the name of Buddha, but only in Jesus' name. (Look up Hebrews 2:14–15.)

Revelation 12:9 tells us of the day when Satan and his angels will be totally defeated. The name of Jesus is powerful because Jesus is God. The demons know it, and that's why they shudder before Him, just as they did when He walked the earth. They knew that He was more than just a man. Look up Luke 8:28, and see the demon's response to Jesus.

The Bible tells us, without a doubt, that Jesus is fully God as well as fully human.

Jesus' Divine Attributes

Here are some things the Bible teaches about the person of Jesus Christ.

Jesus Is Eternal

Jesus is not a created being—He has always existed. Look up Revelation 1:8; Alpha and Omega are a way of saying "the beginning and the end." Jesus was there at the beginning and will be for eternity. He was not created (also see Micah 5:2).

Jesus is the eternal God. For all of eternity He has been the Son, the second person of the Trinity. He has never experienced a beginning. No angel, including Satan himself, can make that claim, for Jesus Christ has created all the angels, and He will also judge them at the end of time. This is why they tremble at His name. Satan hates the name of Jesus because he knows that Christ, the eternal God, will one day throw him into the lake of fire.

Jesus Is the Creator-God

In Colossians 1:16–17 we learn that all things were created through Him. Everything that exists—the earth, the sky, the stars, the planets, the incredible beauty of creation—all these things were created "through him and for him" (NLT). This means that when Genesis 1:1 tells us that "In the beginning God created the heavens and the earth," it is talking about Jesus Christ. He is the Creator-God.

Jesus Directly Claimed to be God

As a Jew, Jesus knew the great admiration His people had for their spiritual father, Abraham. One day, while talking to the Jewish leaders, He made an incredibly bold statement—He claimed to be older than Abraham (who had lived two thousand years before Christ). (Look up John 8:56–59.) This is an amazing statement on the part of Jesus, for not only is He claiming to be older than Abraham, but He does so by saying the words *I am*. To us this may sound a little weird. To the Jews, however, this was blasphemy, for "I AM" is the name of God (see Exodus 3:14). In essence, Jesus was saying, "I am the eternal God of the universe, the God of your forefather Abraham."

For a Jew, those were fightin' words. They picked up rocks in order to stone Him, for in their day, blasphemy was a capitol offense. Anyone who claimed to be God was immediately stoned to death.

Jesus Was All-Powerful

One instance of this was when He spoke to a storm and it immediately stopped raging. (Look up Matthew 8:24–27.) Only God has authority to make the winds and the seas obey. Not only did He display His power over the elements, but He raised a young girl from the dead, changed water into wine, and multiplied five loaves of bread and two fish to feed five thousand people at one time. The power of Jesus is infinite and beyond our comprehension.

Jesus Is Omnipresent

Jesus told His disciples that He would never leave them—He would be with them always. The same promise holds true for us as well. (Look up Matthew 28:20.) As we look at the pages of the Bible, there is never a doubt that Jesus is fully God. He is not created, nor is He less than the Father. He is to be fully worshiped, obeyed, and loved as God.

What an awesome thing that Jesus allows Himself to be known by you and me!

Small Group Discussion

1. Why is it important for you to understand that Jesus is God?

2. Describe what you believe to be the strength in the name of Jesus.

3. Can the power of any demon overtake your life when you have the name of Jesus to call upon? Why or why not?

The Humanity of Christ

Have you ever wondered whether Jesus Christ was fully human? We know that He is God, the second Person of the Trinity, but just how human was He?

Some try to solve the problem this way:

Jesus is 50 percent human.

+ Jesus is 50 percent God.

= Jesus is half God, half man.

This equation sounds good and seems to make good sense—until we look at the biblical evidence. You see, the Scriptures tell us that Jesus was *fully human* and *fully God*. This means that the equation really looks like this:

Jesus is 100 percent human.

+ Jesus is 100 percent God.

= Jesus Christ is fully God and fully man.

Let's look at some aspects of His humanity, aspects that show us that Jesus Christ can fully relate to you and me in our human condition.

Jesus Was Born of a Woman—Mary

Being born is a pretty human thing to do. Chances are good that every person you know was born in the same way—of a woman. When Jesus was born, His mother had real labor pains and a real delivery, just like every other woman who has ever had a baby. Jesus entered this world through a birth canal, just like you and I.

CHAPTER 14

A father was anxiously awaiting the birth of his firstborn child. He just knew that the baby was going to be a gorgeous child, but much to his surprise, the baby boy had a conehead when he was born and actually looked kind of ugly. As is the tradition, the father took the baby from the doctor and reluctantly showed him to the mother, thinking, *Well, good or bad, here he is.* What he didn't know was that misshapen heads are perfectly normal for newborns.

Still a little embarrassed at his baby's "deformity," the dad went to show off his new son. At the viewing window, he held his son up for all to see. He could read the questions in the eyes of his friends, so he mouthed through the glass, "He'll get better; the cone will go down." His friends responded with a sigh of relief.

Yet as the dad held his little son in the nursery, pretty soon the looks of the child didn't matter anymore. This was his son, and he realized he loved him no matter what he looked like. (Later on, of course, the baby's head evened out, and today the child is a handsome young man.)

Maybe Jesus had a misshapen head when He was born, as many babies do. Certainly He cried when He was hungry, and He often needed his diapers changed. From all appearances, He must have appeared to be a normal, happy baby. Of course on the inside there was no sin nature—He was born of a virgin, which meant that He did not inherit the sin nature of Adam—and as He grew He must have had a sweet and obedient attitude toward His parents. The fact is, however, He was a normal child in many ways.

Jesus Learned Things

Look up Luke 2:52. This verse tells us of the young Jesus who grew from boyhood into manhood. In essence it says that Jesus grew intellectually, physically, spiritually, and socially. In all aspects of humanity, Jesus grew and developed just as we do.

How can that be? If Jesus is God, then how could He possibly learn anything? Wouldn't He know everything already?

Read Philippians 2:5–8. Apparently Jesus was willing to *lay aside the privileges of His deity* so that He might fully enter into the experience of being human. He did not cease to be God, but for a limited time He laid aside certain attributes that were inherently His from the beginning. At times, He used those attributes as the Father led Him. For instance, He healed people supernaturally, He could read people's minds, and He could prophecy about the future. Yet these did not take away from His humanity—Jesus was fully human.

Imagine what it must have been like to be Jesus' childhood friend:

- You would have gone to Hebrew school together and studied the Torah, the books of Moses. Jesus' keen insight into spiritual things would have both delighted and amazed your teachers.
- He would have had an incredible ability to learn new things due to the fact that sin would not have clouded His intellectual capabilities as it has ours.
- He would have had an incredible respect for His parents. Never once would you have seen him complain about or disobey His parents.
- He would never have told a dirty joke or hurt someone with silly talk or gossip.
- He would have worked hard and become skilled as a carpenter, learning from His stepfather, Joseph.
- He would have been the best friend you could ever imagine, in every way possible.

Jesus experienced all the phases of life: He learned to walk, He got and then lost baby teeth, He played soccer and other childhood games. He probably even got zits on His nose. Yet none of this detracts from who He is; rather, it helps us understand that Jesus was fully human.

Jesus Experienced All of the Human Emotions

If you've ever lost a friend or a loved one to death, you know that the pain is unbelievable. It's comforting to know that Jesus can relate to this kind of experience. Most likely, He lost His stepfather, Joseph, while He was still a child or young man. There is also the story of Lazarus, one of Jesus' best friends. Lazarus died, and when Jesus arrived at the house, His friend had been dead for four days. As Jesus stood outside the tomb, the Bible says this simple phrase: "Jesus wept" (John 11:35). It's such a simple phrase, but it is packed with significance. The ancient word that's used for "wept" clearly implies that Jesus shed tears for His friend. It may be that He sobbed uncontrollably—we don't know. But we do know that Jesus understands our pain, even when we are shedding tears over the loss of a friend or a loved one.

The Bible also tells us of other emotions that Jesus experienced: joy, compassion, fatigue, and the feeling of being overwhelmed. In all of these things, He proved that He was fully human.

Jesus Did Not Call Attention to Himself

We know this is true because of an event that took place early in His ministry, when He was about thirty years old. In Matthew 13:54–58, Scripture tells us that the people who were astonished at Jesus' ministry were the very people around whom He grew up. His friends, His teachers, the butcher at the corner shop, the vegetable vendor in His neighborhood—all were amazed when Jesus claimed to be the Messiah, the Son of God.

Their reaction tells us that in many ways Jesus appeared to be a very ordinary human being. Although Mary knew the truth because she remembered the circumstances of His birth and the message from the angel Gabriel (see Luke 1:26–2:19), others who grew up around Him were obviously surprised that He was the Son of God. Even his brothers doubted Him. When Jesus told them He was the Messiah, they thought He was crazy and responded sarcastically that He should go out and prove Himself: "His brothers therefore said to Him, 'Depart from here, and go into Judea, that Your disciples also may behold Your works which You are doing. For no one does anything in secret, when he himself seeks to be known publicly. If You do these things, show Yourself to the world.' For not even His brothers were believing in Him" (John 7:3–5).

For the first thirty years of His life, Jesus did not call attention to Himself. He did not seek to impress His friends with miracles or try to outdo them with His supernatural powers. Instead, He lived an ordinary life in perfect obedience to His earthly parents and to His heavenly Father. In all ways, He was fully human.

Jesus Was Tempted in All Things, Yet Without Sin

Read what it says about Jesus in Hebrews 4:15.

Have you ever been tempted by greed? Jesus was as well. Have you been tempted by lust or wrong desires? Jesus knows all about it. Have you felt the lure of this world and the desire to live for wealth, wanting everything that comes from a self-centered lifestyle? Jesus has, for Scripture says that He was tempted in *all* things.

Yet—and this is crucial for us to understand—He never gave in! *Never.* Not even once did He submit to the temptations that surrounded Him. In fact, Satan did his best to lure Jesus into sin while Jesus fasted in the desert (read Luke 4:1–13), yet to no avail.

Every time a student named Jake entered a store, he would browse the aisles looking at the many items he couldn't afford. Jake wanted some of those things so badly that he began to shoplift on a regular basis. At first the items were insignificant and small, but as time went on, they grew in value. Jake became proficient at stealing and even prided himself in his ability. As a believer, he knew it was wrong; but when tempted, he seemed unable to help himself. Eventually he gave up trying to resist. For years Jake struggled with the sin of stealing.

Then one evening God convicted Jake as he was reading the Word. Jake realized the seriousness of what he had been doing, and from then on he began to seek help from friends who would keep him accountable. Over time, he was able to have victory in this area of his life.

Can Jesus understand what Jake was going through? Yes, in the area of temptation. Jesus, however, was unable to sin because He was God. His human nature never existed apart from His divine nature, and the Bible tells us that God cannot sin

(Matthew 5:48). Nonetheless, Jesus understands the lure of temptation against humanity because He experienced it Himself.

Jesus Will Live Forever in a Glorified Human Body

When Jesus ascended into heaven, He did so in a body that is a prototype of the kind you and I will have in heaven. Although He will reign as King of kings and Lord of lords for all eternity, He apparently will never lose the nail scars from His hands and His feet because of the fact that He is *fully human* as well as *fully God*. It will be a constant reminder of the sacrifice He made for our salvation.

Don't ever give in to sin because you think to yourself, *Well after all, I'm only human.* Jesus was human, too, yet His example is one of self-sacrifice and total submission to the Father. We are to model our lives after the life of Christ. (Read 1 John 2:6.)

Kevin loves the Lord, and it shows in how he spends his time. Twice a week he spends time at a downtown homeless shelter where street people come in for food and conversation. He does this willingly because he knows that by doing so he's walking in the footsteps of Jesus.

One evening an older man named George came in from the cold. As Kevin talked with him, it became apparent that the man was at the end of his rope. George had recently lost his only living relative, and he was feeling as lonely as one could ever imagine. Kevin ended up in a two-hour conversation with George, telling him all about how Christ could make a difference in his life. Kevin invited George to church the next day, and he agreed to go.

The next morning George sat in church and heard of the forgiveness and hope that are found in Christ. At the end of the service, he got up from his seat, ran to the front, and fell weeping at the stage. Kevin wrapped his arms around George and led him in a prayer to receive Christ as his Savior.

By loving George, Kevin was following the example that Jesus gave us two thousand years ago. By the power of the Holy Spirit within us, we can all live a life that follows in Christ's footsteps.

Remember that Jesus understands your temptations, fears, and weaknesses. He was fully God, yet fully man.

Small Group Discussion

1. As you pray to Jesus, can He relate to your life as He hears your prayers?

2. Since we are to model Christ, what are some action steps you can take by which you can follow His earthly example (i.e., taking care of the poor and needy, etc.)?

Sin

If you order coffee these days at a McDonald's drive-through window, you'll notice a big, bold warning on the side of the cup: *"Warning: the contents of this cup are very hot and may cause burns if spilled!"*

That seems like a no-brainer, doesn't it? Most people are aware of the fact that coffee is served hot, and hot liquid will cause burns if it's spilled. So why the warning?

I remember reading a newspaper article about a person who spilled McDonald's coffee, got burned, then sued McDonald's because the coffee was "too hot." Instead of taking responsibility for his or her own mistake, this person decided to be the victim, and McDonald's ended up paying millions of dollars to settle the lawsuit.

In a similar case, a friend of mine who works as a state patrolman told me of a man who is suing the state of Oregon for negligence. The man claims that the state police should have spotted him driving drunk before he ran his car off the road and into a telephone pole. In his mind, he was not at fault—the police were to blame.

Here's another one. A guy got drunk at a local tavern and decided to walk home at two in the morning. Somehow he ended up walking in someone's front yard, where he stepped and slipped on a curb and broke his leg. He then sued the homeowners for negligence, even though he had no right to be walking through their yard in the middle of the night.

Does any of this sound familiar? It should because all of us are guilty of making excuses when it comes to our behavior. When caught doing something wrong, it's our nature to blame someone or something else instead of taking responsibility. It is like the eight-year-old who disobeyed his dad by taking his dad's tools out into the field near their house. When the tools were found, the dad confronted his boy: "Son, I told you not to take those tools out of the garage and into the field. Why did you do it?"

The son replied, "But Dad, I didn't do it—*my arm* did it!"

The boy was dead serious—he wasn't about to take the responsibility (and punishment) for disobeying his dad; therefore, he found something else to blame: his arm. As crazy as this sounds, it's not uncommon for any of us to make up excuses—and sometimes our excuses are pretty creative!

Adam's Sin Has Become Our Sin

In the story of Adam and Eve, sin came to us as a result of this couple's choice in the Garden of Eden (read Genesis 3:1–13). Satan planted a seed of doubt in their minds by appealing to their desire to have freedom of choice: "Did God really say you shouldn't eat of the fruit?" he sneered. "Why, God knows that if you eat of it, then you will become like Him, and God doesn't want that. God's command is holding you back from experiencing the wonderful knowledge of good and evil."

Of course, they took the bite—and immediately found that the knowledge they gained was destruction and death. This is how sin entered our world, and ever since we have paid the price for their mistake.

But if Adam and Eve were the ones who took the bite, then why are we punished for their act of sin? Shouldn't we be given the same choice? Actually, we are held accountable for sin because we confirm their choice every time we decide to disobey God. (Read Romans 5:12 and 18–19.)

Like it or not, the human race has been infected with this disease called sin. You caught it from your parents, who caught it from their parents, and on and on. It's like a deadly virus that spreads from person to person—every one of us has inherited its damaging effects. You and I are held accountable because God has justly "imputed" Adam's sin to our account. In other words, when Adam sinned he represented the entire human race. Thus, we are guilty of sin just as Adam was. We are born with a tendency toward sin because we are born with a sin nature. Every time we choose to sin, we confirm the fact that we are like our forefather Adam.

A person doesn't become a sinner only when he or she commits their first sin sometime after they are born. No, the Bible says that we are "conceived" in sin. Psalm 51:5 says, "Behold, I was brought forth in iniquity, and in sin my mother conceived me."

It's useless to say that the corrupted nature we've received from Adam is unfair. The fact is, you and I would have done just what he and Eve did. Each of us stands guilty before God, and each of us is responsible for the choices we make in this life.

What Is Sin?

The Bible uses several different images to tell us the meaning of sin, but one of the clearest is that of an arrow missing the mark. Perfection would be like hitting the bull's-eye every time. In reality, however, we never hit the center of God's perfection. We are constantly "missing the mark."

Sin is the result of our failure to conform to God's moral law. Oftentimes we break God's moral rules on purpose. We know that God has told us to not be immoral, yet we may find ourselves doing something that is morally inappropriate.

Read 1 John 3. Every time we sin we violate God's holy character. At their root, the sins we commit are a personal affront to the One who created us and loves us. This is why God takes sin so seriously.

The Consequences of Sin

In the Garden of Eden, God promised the first man and woman that if they ate of the fruit, "[they] shall surely die" (Genesis 2:17). Can you imagine how they must have felt when they heard God calling for them after they had taken the bite? (Look up Genesis 3:8–9.)

No wonder they were afraid! They remembered God's promise about death, and they weren't anxious to meet their fate. Yet God didn't meet them with a death warrant; instead, He ordered them to leave the garden and told them of several curses that would be theirs as a result of their sin (see Genesis 3:14–19).

Did God lie? Did He go back on His word? No, death just took a different form from what they were probably expecting. Let's look at the different ways death entered Adam and Eve's—and our own—world.

First, they experienced the death of their perfect relationship with God. No longer were they innocent and pure, as He was. No longer could they approach Him as they had before. Their sin was now an obstacle between them, hindering their relationship with God.

Second, they experienced the death of their own innocent relationship. Before the "Fall" (which is what the apple incident is called), both Adam and Eve were naked and unashamed. (Read Genesis 2:25.) They had nothing to hide from each other; their relationship was open, pure, and totally uninhibited. After sin entered the world, however, things were different between them. (Read Genesis 3:7.)

Third, they experienced a death of their perfect environment. Their sin affected more than just the human race; it resulted in all of nature being thrown out of balance. Before the Fall there was no death and no shedding of blood. All of nature was in perfect harmony and balance. After sin came, however, the environment experienced a downward spiral of destructive forces that continue even today. Earthquakes, volcanoes, hurricanes, and many other natural disasters are now commonplace on this planet—all the result of sin.

Fourth, they began their slow descent into physical death. From the moment they bit the apple and left the Garden, Adam and Eve began to experience the effects of sin upon their mortal bodies—aches and pains, blisters, sicknesses, and eventually old age and death. Before sin, none of these things was a reality; now, however, each is a fact of life.

The Corruption That Sin Brings

The Bible tells us that sin is universal—it has affected all of humankind to the very core of its existence.

Look up Romans 3:9–10 and Ephesians 2:3. Maybe you're thinking, *Hey, that's not me; I'm a pretty decent person.* When we compare ourselves with other people, we may look pretty good. When we compare ourselves with God, however—He who is perfect and holy and without any hint of sin—then it's obvious that we are fully corrupted by sin.

The atmosphere in the courtroom was tense, like a coiled spring ready to explode at the slightest touch. Two families had gathered for the sentencing trial, sitting on either side of a wide aisle that divided them. As Marty rose to face the judge, sobs were heard from both sides of the room. Marty had been convicted of killing a teenage girl while driving under the influence of alcohol. Now it was time for his sentence to be handed down.

Before the judge gave the verdict, however, he asked if the victim's family would like to say anything to the young man. The moments that followed left no eyes dry in the giant courtroom.

First the girl's aunt stood up and faced the defendant. She looked him square in the eyes and said, "I hate you. I hate you and I hate your family. You've taken away my niece, and for that I wish you'd never been born."

One by one, other family members stood before Marty and told him how his carelessness had ruined their lives. Some spoke with hatred and bitterness; others, with a sense of mercy for him and his family. Yet all of them spoke of their desire to see him punished severely.

After the victim's family had spoken, the judge then handed down his sentence. Time in prison. The sentence was severe, and the girl's family felt vindicated by the fact that his punishment was fitting for the crime he'd committed.

Now imagine if the judge had decided not to punish the young man. What if the judge had said, "Well, I think this young man is actually a very nice boy, and I don't believe he'll ever do this again. Therefore, I'm going to let him go home without any penalty."

The girl's family would have been outraged, and so would you if you were a part of that family. The reason? Sin is something that must be dealt with. To not do so is to betray a sense of justice that we all share.

In the same way, God must judge sin if He is to remain holy and just. Sin is not something He can leave unpunished, just as the judge could not leave the young man unpunished in the above story. God must punish sin, and God will punish sin. He has no choice in the matter.

No matter what we may think, sin is a serious matter.

Small Group Discussion

1. Describe a situation when you came up with a horrible excuse in order to cover up a sin. Why did you work so hard to cover up your sin?

2. Make a list of some of the sins you see in the world around you. Where did all of these sins come from? Can a person be without sin? Why or why not?

Justification

Sometimes life is extremely unjust. It was in the case of a little boy named Christian.

Mary, a single mom, loved her son more than life itself. Her three-year-old, Christian, was her overwhelming delight in life, and she tried to care for him as best she could.

Christian was an active little boy who loved to run, play, and romp. This didn't bother Mary, but Mary's unstable boyfriend, Jim, often found himself agitated by Christian's behavior. Not only was the boy a handful to take care of, but Jim decided that Christian was getting in the way of his and Mary's relationship.

He decided to do something about it.

The rest of the story is a tragedy beyond description. One day while Mary was napping, Jim took little Christian to an abandoned house across the street and tortured him to death. When Mary woke up and couldn't find her little boy, she quickly alerted the police. For more than a week the city searched for little Christian, with Jim pretending to help in the hunt.

Eventually the body was found, and Jim confessed his crime to the police. Mary's pain became indescribable—not only was her beloved little boy gone forever, but now she learned that her trusted boyfriend was the murderer.

As the shock of these horrible events transitioned slowly from nightmare into daily reality, Mary became consumed with one thing—one thing that might lessen the pain, one thing that *must* take place if the world were a place where she could continue living.

One thing. Justice.

CHAPTER 16

Mary needed a sense of justice in this horrifying situation. She was not vindictive or mean; she just needed to see Jim punished for what he had done to her son, her life, her world. Without justice, Mary was left with nothing.

Without justice, this world would make no sense. Our innate sense of fairness demands that this be the case.

What Is Justification?

By nature, you and I believe that Jim deserved punishment for the above crime. Many of us would say he deserved the death penalty. There must be a fitting consequence to his crime, or evil will have gained an even greater foothold in the world.

Because God is a holy and just God, He will punish sin, just as Jim's crime had to be punished. If God did not punish sin, He would be evil, just as a government would be inherently evil if it refused to punish Jim. In Proverbs 17:15 it says, "He who justifies the wicked, and he who condemns the righteous, both of them alike are an abomination to the LORD."

The word *justification* is a Bible word, and it has everything to do with how God allows people to join Him in heaven. In order for you and me to be saved from our sin, we must first become "justified" in God's sight.

The word *justification,* as used in the Bible, is a legal term. Think of it in terms of a courtroom, complete with a judge, a defendant and his attorney, and a prosecutor. Picture yourself standing as the defendant before God. You wince as the charges are read against you because you know that every one of them is true. You are guilty, with no excuse.

If you were in such a courtroom, what kind of charges would be read against you? Hopefully nothing as serious as what Jim did in the above story. No, if you're like most people, the bad things you've done would pale in comparison to such a heinous crime.

Yet God says that our sin, any sin, is a capitol offense worthy of death. In Romans 6:23 we read these words: "For the wages of sin is death."

Now read Romans 3:23. Who has sinned against God? "All have sinned."

Why is sin worthy of death? After all, didn't God make us the way we are? Why can't He accept us into heaven even though we're not as perfect as He is? It seems intolerant of Him, to say the least.

In reality, God did not make us the way we are—sinners. He created us perfect, in a perfect environment—the Garden of Eden. When Adam and Eve chose to disobey Him by eating of the forbidden fruit, in essence they were making the choice for all of us, a choice that you and I confirm on a regular basis by our daily actions.

Sin is highly offensive to God. He is holy, perfect in every way. In the Old Testament Book of Habakkuk, it says of God:

"Thine eyes are too pure to approve evil,
And Thou canst not look on wickedness with favor."

The simple truth is this: God hates sin. He doesn't play with it, coddle it, or wink at it. And those who sin are under His judgment and worthy of sin's penalty: death. You and I may not like the rules; we may not agree with the rules or even understand the rules. But God is the one who sets the rules according to His holy and just standards.

And according to God, every one of us is guilty of sin and thus worthy of death. Period.

What Does It Mean to Be Justified?

Now picture yourself back in the courtroom once again. You are standing before a holy God who has just pronounced you guilty. The gavel has fallen and its echo reverberates through the massive courtroom. There is no discussion, no debate, and no excuse. You know that the verdict is just, and any attempt to challenge it would be meaningless. Excuses would be futile in front of the One who knows every word, every thought, every motive. Even the best things you've ever done are no match for the stain of sin that covers your soul.

You stand and wait for the sentence. It comes like a swift sword, cutting as deep as bone and marrow. With combined shame and terror you listen as your worst fears are confirmed— you are sentenced to an eternity of death and darkness. There will be no hope for release or parole, no time off for good behavior. You will spend forever paying off the debt that before this moment you took so lightly—the debt incurred by a lifetime of sin.

You close your eyes and tense your body as you await the grasp of the jailer. You can hear the screams and sense the claustrophobic darkness of where you're headed. Your knees begin to buckle out of fright. Yet as you fall, you are suddenly steadied by a strong, gentle presence at your side.

Your eyes open to find a robed figure next to you. His voice is loud and strong as He speaks to the court.

"Father Judge, I am willing to pay the debt that this sinful one has incurred. I have borne eternal death in his place on the cross, allowing him the opportunity to be a forgiven one if he so chooses."

The eternal Judge fixes His gaze on you and responds, "The debt must be paid. Either you must pay it yourself or allow my Son to credit His righteousness to your account, thus paying your debt in full. It cannot be earned—this gift is yours to accept or reject.

"What is your choice?"

What about Our Good Works?

David had a hard time with the message of Christ. Every time he thought about God he felt guilty, so he decided to stay as far away from church as possible. He used to tell his friends that if he ever entered a church building, the walls would fall down from the shock of him being there!

David rationalized his "lack of religion" by comparing himself with other people. "I'm just as good as the next guy, maybe even better," he would tell himself. But truth be told, David wasn't such a great guy after all. For many years he had been having immoral sexual relationships with young ladies in their teens. He knew that what he was doing was wrong, but out of shame and guilt, he covered up his sins. The girls never told on him, and no one else knew about his actions. Still, this was the guilt that David had to live with.

On his deathbed, David remembered the message of Christ. Deep inside himself, though, he didn't feel like he had been good enough to receive salvation. He couldn't bring himself to accept Christ's free gift, so he died without having his sins forgiven. Now, according to God's Word, *David is for all of eternity paying for the sins he committed in this life because he did not accept the gift that was offered to him.*

If you choose to accept Christ's offer, God will declare you justified. It doesn't mean that you are not guilty. It means that *in spite of being guilty,* your punishment is borne by another. Though worthy of death, the blood of Christ has cleansed you from all of your sins. In this way God's wrath is satisfied by the righteousness of Christ being credited to your account.

Justification can only be received as a free gift; it can never be earned! The truth of this goes against our human nature. The apostle Paul was a man who tried very hard to be a faithful follower of God. He was zealous to do good deeds, and when he compared himself to other religious leaders, he always came out on top.

Paul was convinced that He was worthy of heaven. He was so convinced of this that He even persecuted those who trusted in Christ for their forgiveness. That is, until He met Jesus Christ in a personal way. Read Ephesians 2:8–9 and see what Paul says about his good works many years later.

Unfortunately, many people try to earn God's favor by keeping God's rules. They look at the laws found in the Bible and take pride in how many of them they can keep. They believe that keeping these laws (which no one can keep perfectly, by the way) will make them acceptable to God.

However, no one can be justified by rules or by laws. (Look up Romans 5:1–2.)

Good works are important, but not when it comes to being justified. Instead, they are a proper response to what God has done in our lives. Once our hearts are changed by the Spirit of God, we desire to live differently than we did before. He then gives us the power to do good things.

God is a God of justice. Though the world we live in is full of injustices big and small, someday God will make everything right.

Small Group Discussion

1. Think of a story or an event from your own life when someone treated you poorly. Have you ever thought to yourself that that person needed to be punished?

2. Is it possible to do enough good works to become righteous in the sight of God?

The Cross

Robert got out of bed and went down to the kitchen before sunrise, as he did every morning. He fixed a cup of coffee and sat down at the kitchen table to read the morning paper. He'd barely read the headlines for the day when the patter of little feet coming down the stairs let him know that his eight-year-old boy was also up before dawn.

James rounded the kitchen corner and bounded into his father's lap, his broad smile the only sunrise his father really needed. The young boy resembled his dad in an uncanny way. Everyone said they were two peas in a pod. Little James even wore jeans and a plaid shirt, just like his daddy.

They both ate some breakfast before James put down his empty plate and said, "Dad, I'm ready to go with you today." James turned and scooted off his chair backward until his feet touched the floor.

"OK, son, let's get your coat." Robert loved this little boy more than life itself, and this morning he was taking James with him to work for the very first time. His son had begged to go along, and today was the big day. He was proud that his little boy wanted to be just like his daddy.

Father and son headed out the door just as the sun broke over the ridge behind them, a burst of orange highlighting the giant railroad trestle to which they were headed. Robert was a railroad man, and for years he had controlled a switch that moved the giant trestle into place whenever a speeding train approached. As soon as the train was safely over the roaring river below, he would then push another button, returning the span to its original position.

Robert reached the little shack where the controls were contained. He busied himself making sure that the gauges and levers were in working order. The clock on the wall let him know that the morning "6:47" from the big city was only four minutes from the bridge. Sure enough, as he shaded his eyes and looked out the window, he saw the morning sun sparkle off the chrome bullet as it sped down the mountain some four miles away.

As Robert headed back to the switch, a thought startled him out of his daily routine: *Where's my boy?* he said to himself, scanning the hut's small interior.

With a sense of panic he rushed outside and looked over the bank toward the rushing river far below. There was his boy, climbing on the giant gears that would soon turn the trestle into place.

"James! James! James!" the frightened father yelled with all his might. He waved his arms, trying desperately to capture his boy's attention. It was all to no avail; the boy was facing the opposite direction, and the noise of the raging river kept him from hearing his dad's frantic screams.

The whistle of the "6:47"—now two minutes from the river— brought Robert's heart to a standstill. Suddenly he remembered the train. Hundreds of passengers would die if he didn't push the switch and turn the trestle into place.

"My boy! My Jimmy," he cried as he took one last glance at his precious boy. He ran to the switch and reluctantly pushed it down, knowing that his son's life was no more as the giant gears pushed the bridge into position.

"I'm sorry little buddy, please forgive me," he whispered, hot tears stinging his weathered cheeks.

Within a matter of seconds, the glistening train was on the bridge, safely speeding toward the other side, smiling passengers waving to the figure of the switchman hunched over in his little shack. They had no idea the sacrifice he had just made on their behalf.

A Real Father, a Real Story

The above story may or may not be true; no one seems to know for sure. However there is another story that is even more amazing—and we know it is true: a real Father gave up a real Son, for real people who were headed for destruction. Read what the Bible tells us in John 3:16.

Now there's a story that is even more dramatic than the first one: God loving people so much that He sent His Son to die in their place!

The Physical Suffering That Christ Endured

The biblical account of Jesus' suffering and crucifixion is not for the faint of heart. Sometimes we get so familiar with the story that we forget *it really happened*. Take a few minutes and read Luke 23:26–43; think how you would feel if these things happened to a family member or to your best friend. Try to imagine the incredible impact of watching someone go through this type of torture.

What a powerful story. Jesus Christ—the God of the universe, who came to earth and joined humanity—is beat up, spit on, kicked and hit, mocked, flogged, made to carry His cross, then nailed to the wood by His hands and feet.

Don't think for a minute that Jesus didn't feel the same kind of pain that a normal man would have felt. He was in physical agony. The *Journal of the American Medical Association* tells us some of the gory details about scourging and crucifixion as a means of torture:

> As the Roman soldiers repeatedly struck the victim's back with full force, the iron balls would cause deep contusions, and the leather thongs and sheep bones would cut into the skin and subcutaneous tissues. Then, as the flogging continued, the lacerations would tear into the underlying skeletal muscles and produce quivering ribbons of bleeding flesh. Pain and blood loss generally set the stage for circulatory shock. The extent of blood loss may well have

determined how long the victim would survive on the cross.

The severe scourging, with its intense pain and appreciable blood loss, most probably left Jesus in a preshock state. Moreover, hematidrosis had rendered his skin particularly tender. The physical and mental abuse meted out by the Jews and the Romans, as well as the lack of food, water, and sleep, also contributed to his generally weakened state. Therefore, even before the actual crucifixion, Jesus' physical condition was at least serious and possibly critical.[1]

Large metal spikes were driven through the wrists and the feet, attaching the victim to the wooden pole and crossbar. It was not uncommon for a person to hang for many hours, even days, on a cross before dying. Crucifixion was not a humane way to kill someone—it was meant to torture a person to death.

Adequate exhalation required lifting the body by pushing up on the feet and by flexing the elbows and adducting the shoulders. However, this maneuver would place the entire weight of the body on the tarsals and would produce searing pain. Furthermore, flexion of the elbows would cause rotation of the wrists about the iron nails and cause fiery pain along the damaged median nerves. Lifting of the body would also painfully scrape the scourged back against the rough wooden stipes. Muscle cramps and paresthesias of the outstretched and uplifted arms would add to the discomfort. As a result, each respiratory effort would become agonizing and tiring and lead eventually to asphyxia.[2]

The report ends the section on crucifixion as follows:

The actual cause of death by crucifixion was multifactorial and varied somewhat with each case, but the two most prominent causes probably were hypovolemic shock and exhaustion asphyxia.

Other possible contributing factors included dehydration, stress-induced arrhythmias, and congestive heart failure with the rapid accumulation of pericardial and perhaps pleural effusions. Crucifracture (breaking the legs below the knees), if performed, led to an asphyxic death within minutes. Death by crucifixion was, in every sense of the word, excruciating (Latin, *excruciatus,* or "out of the cross").[3]

Basically, this is saying that in spite of all the pain caused by being scourged, beaten, and pierced through with metal spikes, the cause of Jesus' death was suffocation and possibly congestive heart failure.

I've often wondered what thoughts were going through Jesus' mind as He hung on the cross. In almost unbearable pain, He easily could have called down millions of angels and wiped out His enemies, even the whole world. Yet He didn't.

He didn't because of His unimaginable love for you and me.

Jesus Bore the Wrath of God upon Himself

For the first and only time in all of eternity, the Father turned His back on the Son, who bore the wrath of God on the cross. Remember, this is the Triune God, who forever and ever has lived in perfect harmony as three equal yet distinct persons. The relationship between them is marked by incredible love and commitment to each other.

Yet at that fateful moment in human history, the Father took the sins of all the world and placed them on Jesus. Every bad word, every bad thought, every murder, every rape, every lustful idea, every sick and perverted wrongdoing—God the Father placed them on the pure and perfect Son and then punished Him as if He had committed each of them Himself. Jesus bore the weight of sin for the billions of people who have lived on this earth and their manifold billions of transgressions.

That's the real torture of the cross. Jesus didn't just die a painful death. He bore the sin and punishment of every human being—and it resulted in a time of separation from His Father God.

That is why Jesus cried out in such anguish, "My God, my God, why have you forsaken me?" (Mark 15:34 NLT). It was the darkest moment of Jesus' existence. He was literally experiencing hell for you, me, and all of humankind.

Even the skies went dark during those hours. How could there be light in the sky when such oppressive darkness was painfully smothering the Son of God upon the cross?

Jesus was the only man who could pay the price for our sins. (Look up Romans 3:25–26.)

What would have happened to humanity had Jesus not paid the price for our sin? The answer is simple: we would live our lives and then go to directly to hell when we die. Hell is a place for those who want to pay the penalty for their own sins—and it will take an eternity to do so. Heaven, however, is a place for those who accept what Jesus did on the cross as a payment for their sin. Notice that those who are in heaven are no better than those in hell. The only difference is that one has chosen to accept Christ and His forgiveness, and the other hasn't. In the eyes of God, sin deserves punishment forever.

The Work of Christ Is Finished on the Cross

In John 19:30 we read that one of Jesus' last statements while hanging on the cross was, "It is finished!" This means more than the fact that Jesus' life was finished or that His physical pain was finished. No, the ancient Greek word that Jesus used has a much greater significance attached to it.

Literally, the word that Jesus used can be translated as "paid in full." When He cried out just before His death, it was a cry of victory! He had done it—just as He had foretold. (Look up Mark 10:45.)

He had paid the price *in full*—never again would He have to endure the cross and its shame. He had accomplished the mission for which He had come to earth—to buy back humanity from sin through the shedding of His precious blood.

Never take lightly the sacrifice of the cross.

Tim was a young man who professed to be a Christian. He had brought many friends with him to youth group over the years, and he seemed to enjoy his walk with the Lord.

Yet Tim had a tremendous desire to be needed and liked. Because of this, he became very possessive of his best friend, Mike. He would become jealous if Mike hung around anyone but him, and he would literally call Mike on the phone and throw a fit. Tim was very insecure.

The night they graduated from high school, Tim decided to celebrate by visiting a gay bar. Sitting at the counter, he was approached by a guy who started paying him the kind of attention he was looking for from his friend, Mike. Tim enjoyed the attention, and before long he found himself in an immoral relationship with his new friend, Dennis.

When Mike heard that this was going on, he went to his friend and confronted him about his sin. Tim was defensive.

"Mike, for the first time in my life I feel at home. I feel like for so long I've never fit in anywhere, but now I'm loved and understood. I've had homosexual tendencies for years, and I've pleaded with God to take them away. He never answered my prayers, so I figure He must not care much about me either way."

It was obvious to Mike that his friend was turning his back on Christ and pursuing a lifestyle that had no place for God. Only time would tell if Tim had ever known Christ in the first place. For the present, he was certainly turning his back on the sacrifice that the Son of God had made on his behalf.

Small Group Discussion

1. If Christ had not gone to the cross in order to pay for your sins, do you think you could still experience God's forgiveness?

2. What causes a person to turn his or her back on the work of Christ on the cross? How does God view such an act of rebellion?

The Resurrection

Tara was a typical high school student. She loved her mom, but sometimes she was embarrassed to go places with her.

What really bothered Tara were the noticeable scars on her mom's hands. Her mom had never told where they came from, but to Tara they were ugly—and Tara wasn't into ugly. She saw the hands of her friends' moms, all well manicured and very feminine, and it made her embarrassed to be with her mom in public.

One evening Tara's mother asked her if she would like to go shopping for some new clothes. At first Tara said she was busy, then she suggested that her mom give her the money and she would go by herself. Her mom was obviously hurt.

"Tara," she said gently, "why don't you want to go out in public with me anymore? Is something wrong?"

Tara took a deep breath. "OK, Mom, I'll tell you the truth. It's your hands—they embarrass me. I love you, Mom, but I'm afraid people will see your scars and think we're weird."

"Tara, honey, I know I've never told you why my hands are scarred. I think now is a good time to talk about it."

Her mother's eyes seemed distant as she relived a traumatic moment from years ago.

"When you were just a baby, I put you upstairs in your crib one afternoon for a nap. Somehow a heater caught fire in the room next to yours, and the fire soon began to spread rapidly. I was able to reach you, but by the time we got back to the stairs, the fire was blocking our exit.

"The only thing I could do was wrap you close to my chest and go through the fire. I

CHAPTER 18

protected you as best I could with my hands and arms. Even though I was burned severely, the most important thing was that you came through the fire without any harm at all. That's why my hands look the way they do.

"And, sweetheart, for you I would do it all over again."

Tara's eyes filled with tears. She grabbed her mother's hands, pulled them to her lips, and began to kiss the scars over and over again. These were the hands that had saved her.

"I'm sorry, Mother; I'm so sorry," Tara said through her tears. The hands she'd once despised now meant everything to her.

In much the same way, Christ's hands bear scars on our behalf. Our hope of eternal life lies in the fact that Jesus Christ died, was buried, then rose again from the dead. Without the Resurrection, we might as well forget Christianity, the Bible, and any kind of personal relationship with God. The fact of the Resurrection is the basis of our new life in Christ.

The Sequence of the Resurrection

After Jesus' lifeless body was taken from the cross and placed in the cold stone tomb, the enemies of Jesus convinced Pilate (the ruler who ordered Christ crucified) to place guards at the tomb entrance. They knew that Jesus had promised to rise from the dead, and though they didn't believe it, they feared that Christ's disciples might steal the body. To them, an empty tomb would be a political disaster.

In Matthew 27:65, it says, "So they went and made the tomb secure by putting a seal on the stone and posting the guard" (NIV). We know from history that this was no ordinary guard; these were Roman soldiers, each of them the equivalent of a fierce fighting machine. They would guard the tomb with their lives, for any Roman soldier caught sleeping on duty would be put to death.

The seal on the tomb was likely a cord that was stretched across the opening and then secured by wax at either end. The seal represented all the authority and power of Rome. No one would dare tamper with this kind of security operation. It would be the modern-day equivalent of well-armed Green Berets guarding an important outpost.

Besides all of this, the rock that covered the tomb was extremely heavy. No person would be able to move it alone. This means that Jesus, if He were still alive, could not have awoken inside the tomb and moved the stone away by Himself.

So now we have the picture: a dead man is taken down from the cross, wrapped from head to toe in burial clothes, laid in a rock cave, and sealed inside by a huge stone at the entrance. On top of all that, a group of heavily trained Roman guards are placed at the entrance to make sure that no one gets in or out.

To those who were watching, this was a no-brainer—the body was going nowhere! Or so it seemed. . . .

He's alive!

Humankind cannot hold down the truth about Jesus being alive. Whole governments have tried to extinguish the truth by persecuting those who believe in Jesus, but to their dismay, it always backfires. The truth of the Resurrection cannot be held down.

Pilate really thought that he could keep Jesus in the grave, but there is no power anywhere that could have kept Jesus from rising from the dead. If every army in the world had surrounded the grave of Jesus, it still would have been impossible to hold Him in the grave.

Isn't the Resurrection Impossible?

There are many people who deny the resurrection of Jesus Christ because, in their view, it doesn't make sense. "No man can rise from the dead; it's scientifically impossible," they say.

The Bible, however, says that the opposite is true: *It was impossible for Jesus to remain in the grave.* This was because God foretold the Resurrection many times over in the Old Testament. And when God says something will happen, it always happens.

Look up Psalm 16:10 in the Old Testament. King David of ancient Israel wrote this psalm, but we all know that David's bones are still in his grave, so he wasn't writing about himself.

This psalm refers to Jesus, predicting Christ's rising from the dead more than a thousand years before it took place.

Imagine what you would have felt if you were present at the tomb on that third day. (Look up Matthew 28:1–8.)

No enemy could conquer Jesus Christ: not death, not the grave, not even Satan himself. No Roman guards, no religious leaders—nothing could keep Christ from rising from the dead. Jesus broke the stronghold of death and became the "first-born from the dead" (Colossians 1:18).

Michael was a young boy who was full of life and energy. His favorite sport was basketball; in fact, he loved to dribble the ball just about everywhere he went. He would often accompany his two sisters to the corner store. As they walked and talked, Michael would bounce the ball mindlessly with one hand.

Tragically, that's how the accident took place. On a fall afternoon, on the way back from their usual walk to the store, Michael lost control of the ball, and it rolled quickly out into the street. Without even thinking, Michael darted after it and was instantly hit by a car going full speed.

The young boy lay on the asphalt, fighting for his life. His sisters screamed hysterically as they ran to get their mom. When she reached him, she held him in her trembling arms, begging God not to take her little boy. As the ambulance arrived, she hoped beyond hope that her son would be all right.

At the hospital the doctors did all they could to save little Michael, but it soon became clear that he wasn't going to make it. Mom made the hardest choice of her life that evening: she gave permission for her son to be unplugged from his life support. As Michael lay dying, she held him once more in her arms until he took his last breath. She gradually felt the warmth of his body begin to fade away. Her hardest moment was that of leaving the room where her son lay still and lifeless. Michael, her young child, was dead.

But wait—that's not the end of the story. Michael's best friend, John, shared some news with the family that gave them hope. John told of a time when Michael had gone to church with him and his family. That evening Michael had heard the story of Jesus for the first time. On the ride home, Michael turned to John and said that he wanted to accept Christ into his life. They prayed right there in the car.

Michael had made a decision that affected his whole eternity. Because he had received the Jesus who was alive from the dead, he, too, would rise from the dead once this life was over. At the sad funeral that followed, Michael's body was lowered into the ground. Michael, however, wasn't there; he was with Jesus in heaven, where he will remain forever and ever.

Michael is alive just as Jesus is alive. Jesus' resurrection abolished the stranglehold of death upon humanity. Those who accept Christ will experience their own resurrection once this short life is over.

What If Jesus Had Not Risen from the Grave?

As we've been saying, the resurrection of Christ is absolutely critical to the message of the Bible. If you take away the Resurrection, you take away the heart of Christianity.

Read 1 Corinthians 15:17–19. If there was no resurrection, then

- we ourselves have no hope of resurrection after this life;
- Jesus was only a good teacher, not the Son of God;
- we would go straight to hell after this life;
- Satan would have won the victory for human souls;
- there would be no such thing as the church;
- there would be no forgiveness of sins; and
- Jesus would be no greater than any other religious leader who is now dead, be it Buddha or Muhammad.

Without the Resurrection we have no resurrection power. (Look up Galatians 2:20.) This means that we're not meant to live the Christian life by our own strength; we are given "resurrection power" by which to live our lives.

Read Romans 6:4. Brian had been walking strong with Christ for a long time. His greatest desire in life was to obey Christ and to share Him with others. That desire was tested, however, when one day, while walking down a city street, he passed some rough-looking men who were sitting on a park bench.

He felt the Lord prompting him to go back and talk to the men about Christ. *What?* he thought to himself. *That can't be You, Lord, telling me to talk to those guys. They look mean. Besides, what would I say?*

Brian continued walking, but the nagging feeling that he should go back and talk to them only got stronger. His pulse quickened, and his knees felt wobbly as he turned around and headed back toward the men on the bench. "What am I going to say?" he prayed to God half out loud.

When he got near the men, he stopped and stood for a moment until they looked up from their conversation. All three had obviously lived a hard life—hollow eyes, creased faces, and needle marks on their arms let Brian know that these guys had lived a good share of their lives on the streets.

"Look, uh, I don't want to bother you guys, but . . . well . . . I just wanted to tell you that Jesus is alive and that He loves you."

Brian winced inside, bracing for rejection, or even worse, a blow to his face.

"Do you really mean that?" asked one of the men. "If that were true . . . ," he left off, not daring to finish the sentence.

Another one of the men chimed in. "Man, I can't believe that you're telling us about this," he said. "We were just sittin' here, all three of us, complaining about how much we hate our lives. What do you mean when you say Jesus loves us?" The man went on to explain the kind of things they were into: one was a male prostitute, another was a drug addict, and the third was an alcoholic.

Brian spent the next hour sitting with them on the bench, explaining from the Bible about the good news of the gospel. He let them know that no matter what they had done, God would forgive them if they would just ask. Though no decisions were made that day, the three men paid close attention to what Brian was saying, and when he left, they thanked him for telling them about Jesus. The point of the story is that Brian had a life-changing message—Jesus is alive!

Remember that you have been bought with a price—the precious blood of Jesus Christ. The fact that Jesus rose from the dead gives you the hope of resurrection power in this life and resurrection to eternal life once you die.

Small Group Discussion

1. Even though you claim to be a follower of Christ, describe a time when you were embarrassed to admit that you were a Christian.

2. Because of the resurrection of Christ, do you know anyone who today is in the presence of God because of the fact that Jesus is alive?

3. Read Galatians 2:20. Do the people at your school and at your home notice a difference in your life because of the resurrected Christ living through you? If not, why?

Eternity

For thirteen years, Rachel graced this earth with her bright and ever-present smile. Her upbeat personality seemed to make the sun shine brighter, even on gray and cloudy days. An energetic teenager, she was on the verge of maturing gracefully into a virtuous young lady, full of beauty and promise.

Rachel was not only graceful; she was also athletic and loved sports. She excelled in both volleyball and track and was a coach's delight, not only for her ability to play but also for her positive attitude.

Rachel had a very special relationship with her parents. Her mom enjoyed her girl beyond words, and they loved to go shopping and talking together whenever they had a chance. Rachel's dad, a man's man, would come home from work each day and sweep his little girl off her feet, pulling her into a giant bear hug. He was a Bible scholar and teacher, and he loved to engage his daughter in conversations about the Scriptures. Sometimes they talked for hours; Dad enjoyed nothing more than seeing his daughter respond to the truth of the Bible.

On Sundays they would go to church and sit together in the worship service. Rachel would pay close attention, engaged in listening to the pastor's message. When it was time for worship, her mom and dad would smile as they watched her out of the corner of their eyes; she was truly learning to worship her heavenly Father, and it brought them great joy.

Little did this family know that Rachel was being prepared for a homecoming—not the type of homecoming that has football games and halftime shows. No, this was an eternal homecoming—Rachel's time to meet her Savior face to face.

It happened while Rachel was at track practice after school on a sunny spring day. While running some sprints around the track, her heart began pounding and racing like it often did. She stopped and took a seat on the track until the pounding subsided. After a few minutes she was feeling better, so she stood up and began to run some more. This time the pounding came back accompanied by violent pain. Rachel said she wasn't feeling well and sat down with a friend before falling gracefully to the track.

That was the day her family's loss became heaven's gain. The ambulance crew did their best to keep her alive on the way to the hospital, but to no avail. On April 8, 2000, at 4:52 P.M., Rachel went home.

Over the next few days and weeks, Rachel's school responded with stunned disbelief. Her friends were beside themselves with grief. "How could this happen to Rachel?" they asked each other. "She was just here with us—she can't be gone."

As friends and teachers tried to grapple with the tragedy, the Lord used Rachel's testimony as a way to let them hear the gospel. Students were gathering together in the halls for spontaneous prayer meetings. Many students who had previously had no interest in God were beginning to ask questions about their own eternal well-being.

One day, ten of Rachel's friends laid flowers at the base of a hurdle on the track. It was at the exact spot where Rachel had died. They began to pray, and before long there were more than one hundred students gathered around them, their heads all bowed in silence. A young man began to share the gospel with the students. When he was done, he asked if any of them would like to come to Christ. Amazingly, many students prayed to receive Christ right there on the track.

God used Rachel's death to bring many people to Christ. When she was here with us, her life was a strong witness for the Lord. In death, God used her in greater ways than anyone could have imagined.

The Certainty of Death

Take a moment and read Ecclesiastes 8:8. Rachel didn't know the time or the hour when she would be called home. Neither do we. It's easy to ignore the fact that death is certain, especially when we're young. Somehow, we hope that if we ignore death, then it will maybe leave us alone.

The Bible, however, tells us to remember that our days on this earth are numbered. Rather than encouraging us to ignore death and eternity, we are told that only those who focus on eternity are able to live this life in a way that pleases God. (Look up Psalm 90:10, 12.)

Rachel's parents think about heaven a lot these days. They used to think about it in technical or faraway terms; now they think of heaven every time they remember their little girl. Mom is waiting for the day when she and Rachel can walk together and have long conversations, just like before. Dad can't wait to sweep her up in his arms and give her a giant bear hug.

That will be an incredible, wonderful day.

The Hope of Heaven

Heaven is where God has His throne. Isaiah 66:1 says:
"Heaven is My throne, and the earth is My footstool.
Where then is a house you could build for Me?
And where is a place that I may rest?"

The Lord is preparing our home in heaven at this moment. In John 14:2, Jesus told His disciples, "In My Father's house are many dwelling places; if it were not so, I would have told you; for I go to prepare a place for you."

The Bible doesn't tell us everything about heaven (probably because it would literally blow our minds), but it does tell us that heaven will be a place of incredible beauty, peace, and perfect joy. There will be no pain or suffering in heaven.

Think of it. Jesus says He left this earth in order to go and prepare a place for us. I wonder what that home will look like. It will make the biggest mansion here on earth seem like a doghouse in comparison.

And believe me, heaven will not be boring! We won't be sitting around on clouds all day playing harps forever and ever. No, heaven will be a place of joyful service to our King and Lord, Jesus Christ.

Heaven—A Place of Reward

Those who have been faithful to "invest in eternity" will be rewarded accordingly, while those Christians who have squandered their lives on selfish gain will experience a loss of reward.

Look up 2 Corinthians 5:10 and Romans 14:10–12. What a sobering thing! God knows every word you've said and every thought you've embraced in your mind. There are no secrets from Him, and someday we will stand before Him and either be rewarded for our faithfulness or lose our reward because of unfaithfulness. (Look up Hebrews 4:13.)

The more you give up to follow Jesus Christ, the greater will be your reward in heaven. In fact, if you're persecuted here on earth for Jesus' sake, God says you should actually rejoice because of it, for "great is your reward in heaven" (Matthew 5:11–12 NIV).

Heaven—Our True Home

Why should we focus on heaven when it seems so far away? Because how we live this life really does affect how we will spend our eternity. Let's look at a few things that are true about heaven.

First, there will be worship in heaven. We get a glimpse of this worship when we read the Book of Revelation. (Look up Revelation 7:9–10.) Jesus will be lifted up and exalted in heaven, as will all the Trinity. We will experience unbelievable worship in God's very presence. There will be the most beautiful songs— things we've never heard before, nor can even imagine. No one will be tone deaf or will sing off-key. And not only will we be singing as a multitude of people, but also the angels will join in and lift their voices. We will never grow weary of singing praises to our God.

Second, we will spend all of eternity learning about God. God is like no other being in this vast universe—He is infinite. That means that we will learn about Him, then learn something more, then more and more and more. This will continue for all of eternity.

Third, heaven is a place of wonderful reunions. When Rachel went home to be with her Lord, she joined all of the millions of people who have gone there before her. (Look up Hebrews 11:40.)

The Bible tells us that when we die we go directly to be with Christ. We understand this from the writings of the apostle Paul in passages such as Philippians 1:23 and 2 Corinthians 5:8.

When you die, you will be able to think and to remember. You will not enter an unconscious state or a place of waiting. Rather, you will be transferred into the very presence of God. You may even be able to see what is happening here on earth. Will you be able to watch your own funeral? We don't really know. But if you could, you would view the service very differently than you view a funeral here on earth. You might see sorrow, but you will be in complete joy.

If heaven seems too far away to be real, then I encourage you to heed Jude's admonition from the Bible. In Jude 21, he says this: "Keep yourselves in God's love as you wait for the mercy of our Lord Jesus Christ to bring you to eternal life" (NIV).

We don't know exactly what heaven will be like. But we do know that God keeps His promises, and God has promised that heaven will be a place of unspeakable joy and unimaginable delight. Again, Paul tells us in 1 Corinthians 2:9:

Just as it is written,

"THINGS WHICH EYE HAS NOT SEEN AND EAR HAS NOT HEARD,
AND which HAVE NOT ENTERED THE HEART OF MAN,
ALL THAT GOD HAS PREPARED FOR THOSE WHO LOVE HIM."

The Opposite of Heaven

We can't talk about eternity and heaven, however, without acknowledging the reality of hell. Though many people choose not to believe in its existence, the Bible is clear that hell exists and that many people will spend eternity in the confines of hell's loneliness and suffering.

Maybe you've heard of a man named Anton Levey. This man considered himself to be the high priest of Satanism here on earth, and he even wrote a book called *Satan's Bible,* a manual on how to worship the devil.

A youth pastor named Doug went shopping at a bookstore in California one day. As he entered the store, he felt something strange come over him. He looked around to see what was going on, and as he glanced at the store's other entrance, he saw a man entering the store who was dressed all in black. Doug knew who it was—it was Anton Levey.

Doug continued his shopping, but the eerie feeling kept getting stronger and stronger. At one point he felt that someone was staring at him. He turned around and there was Levey, staring right at him with an evil gaze. Doug knew that this man had given himself over entirely to evil, and he didn't want to mess with the powers of darkness. He turned and ran out of the store, which was probably the wisest move he could have made.

Since then, Anton Levey has died. If it's true that he never received Christ, one can only imagine the eternity that he will experience in Satan's presence. The evil and darkness that he immersed himself in for a lifetime here on earth will be his in fullest measure. He is now experiencing utter darkness and complete separation from God for all eternity.

Hell is a place that was originally created for Satan and the angels who joined him in rebelling against God. We are told in Matthew 25:41, "Then He will also say to those on His left, 'Depart from Me, accursed ones, into the eternal fire which has been prepared for the devil and his angels.'"

God's original plan never involved people going to hell; He created humankind to dwell with Him in His heaven forever and ever. When man sinned against God, however, the justice of God demanded that there be consequences for that sin. And we know from the Bible that the "wages of sin is death" (Romans 6:23).

Hell is a place of death—where people experience the death of any possible relationship with God, the death of any happiness they might have had, and the death of any possible future fulfill-ment. There are no second chances—it is a place of finality.

The Bible also tells us that hell is for all of eternity. Look up Revelation 19:3 and Isaiah 66:24. These are just two passages in the Bible that tell us that hell will last forever. Hell is not a place where a friend can sit and have coffee with his buddies while talk-ing about the good old days. In hell, we know that there will be darkness, suffering, and complete isolation. Hell is a place where God will remove every good thing.

Yet hell will not be the same for all who are there, just as heaven will be enjoyed differently by those who receive greater or lesser rewards. Revelation 20:12–15 describes how people will receive various degrees of judgment depending on the deeds they have done:

> And I saw the dead, the great and the small, standing before the throne, and books were opened; and another book was opened, which is the *book* of life; and the dead were judged from the things which were written in the books, according to their deeds. And the sea gave up the dead which were in it, and death and Hades gave up the dead which were in them; and they were judged, every one *of* them according to their deeds. And death and Hades were thrown into the lake of fire. This is the second death, the lake of fire. And if anyone's name was not found written in the book of life, he was thrown into the lake of fire.

Those who die without receiving Jesus Christ as their Savior and Lord will receive a just punishment from God. The Bible tells us that God does not delight in punishing anyone (Ezekiel 33:11), but instead desires that everyone would find eternal life. The reality is, however, that God has given men and women the freedom to choose. C. S. Lewis puts it this way: "There are only two kinds of people in the end: those who say to God, 'Thy will be done,' and those to whom God says, in the end, '*Thy* will be done.' All that are in Hell chose it."[1]

Do what you can to tell others about Christ and the reality of His love for them. In doing so, you will be following the advice of Jude 23: "Snatch others from the fire and save them" (NIV). There's nothing greater you can do for a friend.

Small Group Discussion

1. Explain the level of your faith in the existence of eternity. How do you know for sure that you will spend eternity with Jesus?

2. Who do you know that is in heaven right now? What do you think they are doing at this moment? What choice did they make in order to end up in heaven?

3. Why do some of your friends deny the reality of hell?

4. Do you know anyone right now who is most likely in hell?

PART 4
Experiencing God

The Power of Friends

Brandon had a gift. He loved sports, and sports loved him. As a star athlete at his high school, Brandon ended up as a starter and key contributor on every team he went out for. His athletic prowess gained him notice with both fans and coaches alike.

That's why his sudden downfall took everyone by surprise. Brandon had never been a rowdy kind of guy, but increasingly he started hanging out with the kind of guys he'd always stayed away from in the past—guys who didn't think twice about breaking the rules, who loved to boast about the trouble they could cause. It wasn't long until Brandon started breaking the rules too.

It was the morning that Brandon came to school drunk when things started to reach bottom. With his head spinning and his stomach turning, he found himself face-to-face with the vice principal in his office. It didn't help that the vice-principal also found some drugs in Brandon's coat pocket. Within a few minutes, the basketball coach was called into the office, and Brandon was off the team. Period.

It took Brandon a few hours to sober up, and then a few days more to realize what a foolish choice he had made.

"Why did I do such a stupid thing?" he chided himself. "I can't believe I'm off the team. This was going to be my big year. How can this be possible?"

Brandon began to review some of the choices that had gotten him to this point. He thought about the friends he had chosen and the path he was following. He knew that if he didn't make some changes he would never play school ball again; and worse, he

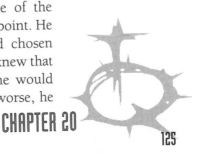

CHAPTER 20

might end up making poorer choices in the future—choices that could carry severe and lasting consequences.

It was during this time of personal reflection that Brandon was invited to attend a church youth group. He didn't know the guy who invited him that well, but since Brandon's evenings were suddenly freed up from games and practices, he decided to go along and see what it was like.

The message he heard hit him right between the eyes. He felt like the speaker was talking directly to him.

"You can make a fresh start," said the pastor from up front. "Jesus Christ can clean you up from the inside out. All you've got to do is invite Him to take over your life and to forgive you for all the things you've done wrong. He'll make you a new person. Guaranteed."

Brandon was ready for a change. He knew that he was sinful and dirty on the inside, so at the end of the talk, he didn't hesitate even a moment to pray a prayer inviting Christ into his life. Funny thing was, he didn't care who saw him go forward and talk to the pastor after the program ended. All he knew was that he felt forgiven. It was as if a weight had lifted off his soul.

Brandon lay in bed that night feeling cleansed and full of joy. He didn't feel dirty anymore. Somehow he felt like a new person. He began to think of some of the guys who he'd been hanging around with and how they could feel this way, too, if they would give their lives to Christ.

The next day he spied a couple of friends who were hunched over a cafeteria table devouring lunch. He crowded in between them and spread them apart with his elbows. "Hey guys," he smiled. "You're not going to believe what happened to me last night."

The two students glanced at each other before one smirked, "Yeah, Brandon, we heard. Sounds like you got religion, dude."

"Preach to us, Reverend," said the other friend sarcastically. "On second thought, don't bother!"

"Yeah, don't bother," echoed the first friend, his mouth full of food. "I don't think you'd make a good little religious boy anyway.

You're too much like us." Both friends laughed, enjoying the silly notion that they would ever end up as "Bible thumpers."

Brandon did his best to hang around his friends, but try as he could, he just didn't feel comfortable with them anymore. Every weekend was the same old thing: drink beer, chase girls, and search for ways to get in trouble. Brandon tried living the old way for awhile, but he always came away feeling dirty.

One day Brandon noticed some kids at school whom he knew were living for the Lord. He began to watch them. In class, in the hall, and at lunch he began to evaluate how they were living. Most of them had a brightness about them; they seemed to really be enjoying life.

In PE class, he started to hang out with one of guys that went to church. Pretty soon he was sitting with this guy and his friends most every day at lunch. He even started spending time with them on the weekends. It didn't take long for Brandon to realize that his new friends were rubbing off on him. They would talk about God, and it actually felt good, not weird. He realized that his language wasn't as foul as before, and as he got involved in the youth group and began reading the Bible on a regular basis, people at school began to comment on how Brandon was changing.

Brandon was different—so much so that one of his old friends, Chris, began to hang around and ask Brandon questions. Soon Chris was going to church with Brandon, and before long Chris also decided to give his life to Christ.

Now the two of them were on fire for the Lord. No longer did they say things like "Let's go drinking Friday night and see what girls we can pick up." Now they spent time reading the Bible together and talking about the Lord. They remained friends with the guys in the old gang, but they didn't preach at them; they just lived a pure life in front of them.

It wasn't much later that another one of their old friends came to Christ. John saw the change in both Chris and Brandon, and his curiosity led him to ask some questions and finally surrender his life to God. Now the three of them were enjoying the Lord together.

All of this change took place in a few short months. The change in Brandon's life was apparent to everyone, including the basketball coach. Brandon was allowed to play basketball the following year. He made honorable mention, and both he and Chris went on to play college ball after graduating from high school.

What is it that will sustain a new Christian and help him or her stay close to God? It's two things: a commitment to reading God's Word and a decision to hang around people who also love Jesus. If Brandon had not made the choice to seek out Christian friends, he would not have grown in the Lord, and he very likely would have fallen away from his faith.

If you are a believer in Jesus Christ, and yet your closest friends are not, it's very likely that your spiritual growth will be hindered, if not stymied altogether. In 1 Corinthians 15:33 we're told that "bad company corrupts good morals." That makes sense when you consider that unbelievers

- often don't share your moral convictions,
- don't have the ability to relate to you on a spiritual level, and
- can't really understand the most important thing in your life, which is Christ.

Mitch was a young man who'd been raised in the church but now found it to be boring. He wanted to find some thrills in life, so he began to search for some friends who lived on the edge of right and wrong. When he started hanging around Tommy, Mitch's parents constantly warned him that he was making a mistake. Tommy had a way of influencing Mitch to do just about anything, and Mitch's parents tried many times to keep them apart, but to no avail.

One afternoon Mitch joined Tommy and another buddy, Mark, on a ride up to a local mountain. When they reached the top, they jumped out of the car and had a brief snowball fight. They were having a good time just messing around when Tommy suddenly got very angry at Mark. Mitch knew that Tommy was unpredictable, but Tommy was angrier than Mitch had ever seen him.

Tommy looked over at Mitch and said, "I hate Mark; I would really like to kill him." Mark didn't hear what had been said, and he started walking toward Tommy. Tommy suddenly pulled a gun out of his pocket, aimed it at Mark, and pulled the trigger. Mark crumpled to the ground—dead.

Mitch couldn't believe his eyes. He thought he was next to take a bullet, but Tommy turned and said, "Quick, let's cover the body and get out of here." Mitch did as Tommy requested, and then the boys drove down from the mountain.

When Mitch was dropped off at his house, he immediately ran upstairs and told his parents. They quickly called the police, and in time both Tommy and Mitch were arrested for Mark's murder. Eventually, after much investigation, Mitch was found not guilty and released from jail.

The important lesson this story teaches is this: *It is absolutely crucial that you pursue making friends with people who are actively following Christ.*

Beware of "Back-Row" Christians

What about friends who say they love Christ, yet their actions are just the opposite? Isn't it possible that a person can be a Christian but just not live it out very well? It is possible, and unfortunately, it happens all the time. Beware of a friendship that doesn't easily center on Christ.

Carnal friends aren't hard to spot. The warning signs are abundant:

- They will want to get as close to sin as possible and will justify doing wrong things.
- They will attend church with a nonchalant, noncaring attitude. Many will sit in the back row, never caring about the message and rarely paying attention.
- They may even mock and laugh at those who are serious about their Christian faith.
- They will claim to be Christians but will be ashamed of following Christ.

How to Be a Godly Friend

Perhaps the best way to find godly friends is to work hard at being a godly friend yourself. Here are some ideas for how to sustain friendships that are pleasing to the Lord.

- Genuinely enjoy talking about Christ with other people. Learn how to bring Him up in natural conversation while talking with others.
- Allow your Christian friends to correct you if, and when, you step out-of-bounds in your Christian walk. Work hard at not being defensive.
- Don't be easily swayed back to your old lifestyle. It will stunt your growth in the Lord and disappoint those who are close to you.
- Be fun to be around. Laugh, have a great time, and develop your sense of humor and the natural abilities and talents God has given you.
- Encourage your friends in the areas where they do well.
- Be active in prayer with, and for, each other.
- Seek out environments together where you can grow spiritually. Let godly places and activities be the hub of your social life and your relationships.

Don't let wrong friendships hinder your new life in Christ. Choose your closest friends carefully. Make sure they are leading you *toward* Jesus Christ, not away from Him.

Small Group Discussion

1. Think of a time when some friends talked you into making a choice you regret to this day. Did they claim to know Christ? What excuses did they offer you for doing wrong?

2. What friends do you have today who have your best spiritual interest in mind? In what ways do they protect you? How much time do you spend with these friends compared to wrong friends?

How to Love Others

Sherri loved the Lord. It was obvious by the way she lived her life, by the words she used, and by her commitment to grow into a godly woman. She was a pretty girl who was gifted with a bright mind and the ability to make friends quickly. Boys were either attracted to her immediately upon meeting, or put off by her high standards when it came to dating and relationships.

In the secret moments, other girls sometimes gossiped about Sherri, trying to bring her down to their level in their own minds. When she heard these things, it made her feel bad. Still, she remained firm in her convictions, content to focus on loving God with all of her heart.

But Sherri's love didn't stop there—she also developed a tremendous love for people. Her friendship with a girl named Gail was an example of this.

Gail was on the other end of the social spectrum from Sherri. Whereas Sherri was pretty and fun to be around, Gail had virtually no friends. She was basically unattractive, and her poor social skills made it difficult for people to be around her. Gail tried so hard—too hard, in fact—to be accepted. Whenever anyone tried to be nice to her, she would latch on to him or her like a leech—literally chasing people away by her obsessive behavior.

Sherri saw Gail and her heart went out to her. She approached Gail one day at school and said, "Hi, Gail. I'm Sherri. I've seen you at youth group on Wednesday nights. I'm wondering if you would like to do a Bible study with me?"

Gail was both flabbergasted and thrilled. "I'd love to," she responded. That was the

CHAPTER 21

beginning of a valuable friendship between two girls who were very different, yet equally valuable to God.

The two girls met together once a week for several months, studying the Bible and talking about who God is and what He is like. For the first time in her life, Gail understood that God loved her and that He had provided forgiveness for her sins through the person of Jesus Christ. It was a thrilling day for both Gail and Sherri when Gail bowed her head and prayed to receive Christ into her heart.

Now the two were more than friends—they were sisters in the Lord. Yet Gail's difficult behaviors didn't change overnight. Sherri gently helped her recognize her quirks and how she came across to people. She told her the truth and helped her set boundaries in their relationship. When Gail would latch on to her new friend too tight, Sherri would say, "Gail, you're my friend, but I have lots of other friends too. You can call me once or twice a week, but not more."

Sherri mentored Gail in how to act around boys too. Gradually Gail began to change, and eventually others began noticing that she was different and easier to be around. Sherri's friendship was a turning point in Gail's life. Gail was forever changed because a popular girl who loved Jesus reached out to her with Jesus' love.

Now, here's the question: what was in this for Sherri? It's obvious how the relationship benefited Gail, but why would Sherri take the initiative to reach out to someone so difficult to be around? After all, there was a cost involved in choosing to hang around Gail—emotionally, socially, and timewise. Sherri wasn't paid to reach out to others, nor did she receive a regular pat on the back from her pastor or others in authority over her. So why even bother to love the unlovely?

The answer is all about love—God's love.

What Is God's Greatest Commandment?

It's hard to love people who, for various reasons, are difficult to even like. For instance, what about the person who really is your enemy, someone who treats you like dirt for no good reason? Or how about the people around us who are needy, or poor, or socially unacceptable?

The Bible says something very interesting about our reaction to these types of people. It's really kind of black-and-white in passages such as 1 John 4:20–21.

This is very similar to what Jesus said to a bunch of people who were concerned about loving God but not concerned about loving people. (Look up Matthew 12:28–29.)

If you were to take the Christian life and boil it down to its simplest elements, there are two commands that would remain above all else: *Love God with all you've got,* and *Love people as yourself.*

Where Does Love for Others Come From?

Steve and Nate were two unbelievers who hated each other's guts. Why? They weren't really sure why—all they knew was that whenever they saw each other in the hallway at school, they had an overwhelming desire to pound on each other.

Steve hated the way Nate laughed, the way he walked, the way he played sports. He disliked everything about the guy. When Nate would raise his hand in class, Steve would think to himself, *I even hate the guy's arm! I can't stand anything about him.*

Then an amazing thing happened: Steve met some Christians who began to share the Lord with him, and eventually he ended up receiving Christ into his life. Steve was so excited, he could barely contain himself. When it came time for his first youth group retreat, he could barely wait to get to the beach and learn more about the God he now served.

On the day of the retreat, Steve arrived at the church parking lot a little bit late. As he tried to squeeze into one of his buddies' vehicles, it became obvious there was no room for him to sit. Then he saw Nate pull into the parking lot. Steve had heard that Nate, too, had recently received Christ into his life and that they would both be on the retreat together.

"Hey guys, I've got a seat available in my car if anybody needs one," Nate yelled at the group.

Again, Steve tried frantically to get a ride with one of his buddies. He tried three different vehicles before he finally realized the obvious—he was going to have to ride with Nate.

With a scowl on his face, Steve grabbed his stuff and walked over to Nate and his car. Without saying a word, he threw his stuff in the backseat, sat down on the passenger side, and closed the door. As Nate pulled out of the parking lot, the silence between them was deafening. Steve knew this was going to be the longest trip of his life.

For a long time neither of them said a word. Then, rather reluctantly, Nate spoke first.

"So you received Christ, huh, Steve?" he said tensely.

"Yeah," Steve replied. When Nate asked him how it happened, Steve began to share his story. Then Nate shared how his life was being changed and how great it was to know the Lord personally. Soon the two were in a deep conversation about what God was doing in their lives. The antagonistic walls between them began to crumble as they talked, and by the time they reached the beach three hours later, their relationship was mended. Incredibly, these former enemies became good friends, brought together by the love of Christ.

Maybe you're wondering how you could ever love some of the people who have hurt you the most. The fact is, you can't do it on your own. Tell God about it. Explain to your heavenly Father how you feel; then ask Him to give you His perspective on the person or individuals who have hurt you so deeply.

What Does Love Look Like?

Love can be defined many ways, but one thing is for sure: love is more than just an emotion. Though it may include feelings, and probably does in most cases, God's love is best revealed by the things He does for those He loves.

Take a few moments to look up John 3:16. Notice that God's love doesn't just stop with an emotion. Thankfully, His love drove Him to do something for the good of the whole world—namely, sending His Son to die for us. That's a great pattern for each of us to follow as we see people around us who have needs.

For instance, some years ago a girl named Julie showed God's love to a large number of children during the Christmas season. Julie is a quiet girl who doesn't enjoy drawing a lot of attention to herself. Still, she has a close walk with God, and she desires to be all that God wants her to be. Therefore, she decided to move out of her comfort zone and do His work.

One year, God gave her the idea of providing Christmas presents to needy children in her city. At her high school she organized a gift drive, and to her delight, other students responded in a big way. It got so big that the program even received attention from the local news stations. For Julie, this was a huge confirmation of how God could use her to reach people with His love. God had obviously moved the hearts of people to care for the needs of others. If Julie hadn't responded to His prompting, it may never have happened.

Remember, according to the Bible, it's impossible to love God without loving people. Draw close to the Father. Be continually filled with the Word of God and with the Spirit of God. As you do, you'll find that God will fill you with His love, even for those people you can't love on your own.

Small Group Discussion

1. Think of persons who rub you the wrong way. How can you supernaturally begin to love them?

2. Who are the people in your life who have modeled love and care for you? How did they show God's love?

Temptation

John knows his way around the computer in his bedroom better than he knows the hallways at school. And no wonder—he spends all his free time with his nose inches away from a seventeen-inch monitor that acts as a window into fascinating travels throughout the cyber-world.

John's fascination with the computer is preparing him well for a possible high-tech career someday. Unfortunately, it also opened him up to hundreds of temptations he never knew existed.

It started one late night while doing research for a term paper for school. His parents and siblings were in bed, and the only light on in the whole house was the eerie monitor glow bouncing off the walls of his bedroom. John had heard that there were seamy areas on the Internet where people shouldn't go, but until that evening he'd never experienced it for himself.

The search engine responded to an innocent query with a number of not-so-innocent links. John ran his mouse pointer over several of them, curious about what lay behind these words— words he knew were full of sin, yet words that enticed and gleamed, stirring within him a powerful urge to indulge the fleshly side of his being.

He stared at the monitor, a battle for good and evil raging in his soul. He could feel his pulse quicken as he considered what forbidden images might lie beyond a simple click of the mouse.

"No one will know. . . . I'm old enough to handle these things. . . . Every red-blooded

American male looks at magazines. . . . I'll just check it out once so I know not to go there again."

With each excuse John could feel the shaky walls of resistance begin to crumble. For a moment he almost snapped back to reality as his conscience reminded him that there are consequences to sin. The thought appeared to him as a lifeline, and he knew his choice was that of grabbing hold and being pulled to personal purity, or sinking into a toxic ocean of fleshly lust.

The intensity of the battle surprised John, as did the fact that he gave in so quickly to the wrong side. With a click of the mouse he found himself exposed to fascinating, alluring pictures that at once repelled and attracted his feasting eyes. Like a drug user seeking an ever greater hit, he clicked his way through an hour or so of glossy pictures until a combination of weariness, guilt, and boredom caused him to finally click off the machine.

Was this the end of the world for John? Not really. He went to school the next day, he got his paper in on time, and life went on as normal.

No, it wasn't the end of the world, but it was the beginning of a struggle. Now there is a new temptation in his life every time he gets on the computer. Not a day goes by when he doesn't experience a strong temptation to visit the dark areas of the Internet once again.

What Is Temptation?

Temptation is the desire to do something wrong, something that we know we shouldn't do. (Read James 1:14–15.)

That's how temptation works. We are enticed by something, or someone, or by a desire that wants to carry us away (the word *lust* means "strong desire" and is often used when referring to wrong sexual desires). If we give in to that temptation, it becomes sin, resulting in spiritual death. This doesn't mean you'll keel over and die if you give in to temptation. It does mean, however, that your sin will affect your walk with God in ways that, over time, can become deadly to your spiritual life.

If you've ever gone fishing, you know how the process works. Have you ever caught a fish by just throwing a bare hook into the water? Probably not, unless the fish are either very hungry or very stupid! No, the skill of fishing has much to do with how to attract the fish, and this attraction has everything to do with the kind of bait you use.

How Does Temptation Work?

Temptation creates a curiosity, then a desire, then a sense of need. In John's life, the lure of pornography became the bait. He knew it was wrong, but after giving in to it several times, he found that he couldn't escape from its trap—he was caught in a web of sin.

This is the way things have worked since the beginning of the human race. It started with Adam and Eve in the Garden of Eden. Read Genesis 3:6 and notice the three things that tempted Eve when deceived by the serpent (the devil in disguise).

When the woman saw that the tree was *good for food*, and that it was *a delight to the eyes*, and that the tree was *desirable to make one wise*, she took from its fruit and ate; and she gave also to her husband with her, and he ate. (italics added)

We find a similar list in 1 John 2:15–19.

Though you may be tempted in different areas than your friends, temptation always works the same way no matter what the bait. In fact, temptation can come in the form of any kind of sin or wrongdoing: greed, pride, jealousy, lying, gossip, sexual immorality, disrespect for authority, laziness, procrastination, alcohol, drugs, etc.

Perhaps you struggle with the issue of going to parties. Before you became a Christian, there was probably no question—you would just go. Now, however, you've got a choice to make, for many of your friends are still drinking and going to parties. You now know it's wrong—not only is it against the law, but it also harms your Christian witness.

How to Resist Temptation

Sometimes the temptations we feel in us and around us make us feel like we're in the middle of a war. In reality, *we are* in the middle of a war—a war for good and evil—and it rages in our souls every day. It is real. It is intense. Yet God has promised us the victory if we follow His prescribed battle plans as described in the Bible. (Look up 1 Corinthians 10:13.)

So how do we resist temptation? *First,* remember that God will never give you a temptation that is greater than you can handle. Every temptation is tailor-made to help you grow, not to leave you defeated.

Second, know that there is always an escape hatch nearby. God will never leave you alone, helpless in the midst of your passions, your anger, or your selfishness. He will always give you a way out—if you choose to take it.

Third, stay away from people or things or places or programs that cause you to be tempted.

Fourth, if you're struggling with a particular temptation, grab a mature friend or a number of mature friends and share with them how you need to be accountable to them.

I know a guy who stopped at a convenience store one time in order to grab a few groceries. After filling his arms with items, he headed to the checkout line, where he found himself having to wait in line right in front of a magazine rack filled with glossy pictures of half-naked women. His first, and most natural, thought was to let his eyes drink their fill of the images that were before him.

Yet almost immediately some words came to his mind: "Flee from youthful lust." He knew that he was thinking of a verse from the Bible (2 Timothy 2:22), and that it was the Holy Spirit helping him remember what he should do. Almost without hesitation, the guy did something that may seem crazy: he set his groceries down on a cart, turned his back to the magazines, walked out of the store, and never came back. He knew that if he waited around much longer, he might do something that would make him sorry later on. He took the Bible literally—he fled from the temptation before he could give in to it.

The truth is, every one of us experiences temptation. It's a consequence of living in a fallen, evil world. The good news is that Jesus can help us in any area in which we struggle.

Don't play with temptation; instead, flee from it. In the long run, you'll be glad you did.

Small Group Discussion

1. In what situations or environments do you experience the most temptation?

2. How do you think God can help you resist difficult temptations in the future?

The God Who Hears You (Prayer)

Bo sat in his youth pastor's office, soaking in the Bible study they were doing together. He never knew that the Bible could be so exciting, so relevant to the everyday things he was experiencing at school, at home, and at his part-time job. He was just beginning to get a glimpse of his newfound heavenly Father.

Their hour together flew by quickly, and the pastor suggested that they end their time by praying to God for a few minutes.

"Bo, how about you pray first, then I'll close," said the youth pastor.

Bo's pulse quickened, and his neck began to feel hot and sweaty. "I don't know how to pray; I've never really talked to God before. I . . . I don't really know what to say."

His older friend smiled. "I know how you feel. I remember feeling that way, too, a long time ago. Actually, prayer is talking to God just as you would talk to another person. Why don't you say thanks for our time together, then tell a couple things that are on your heart. I'll take it from there."

"OK, I'll try," Bo said nervously. He wasn't sure why he felt so uncomfortable; he'd heard other people say prayers lots of times. It's just that he'd never thought about what *he* would say to God. *After all, what are you supposed to say to the King of the universe?*

"Umm . . . Father . . . ," Bo stammered nervously. "Father, I want to serve you, and . . . uh . . . I want to be a strong Christian."

CHAPTER 23

He could feel himself sweating, and he began to fidget a little as he searched for words. He continued trying to put thoughts into words.

"Anyway, God . . . I'm glad to be Your child. And, well, I guess that's it for now."

He looked up into the grin of his youth pastor. "Hey, that wasn't as hard as I thought it would be. That felt good!" Bo said through a smile.

How Do We Pray?

It does feel good to pray, mainly because you and I were created to be in a close relationship with the God of the universe, and it's hard to be close to someone when we don't talk to him or her very often.

That's what Jesus taught a bunch of new believers who hung around with Him for three years during His earthly ministry. These twelve guys, whom we know as the disciples, watched Jesus relate to His Father personally and intimately. They watched Him pray as if the Father was sitting with them around the campfire or walking with them along dusty roads.

One day they asked Jesus an all-important question: "How do we pray?" They wanted to relate to the Father as Jesus was relating to the Father. They wanted to converse with the God of the universe, but they weren't quite sure how to start the conversation.

Have you ever wondered the same thing? Maybe you've seen or heard your friends talking to God, but you've never really learned how to pray on your own. Some people sound so official—so scripted—when they pray. Others make it sound as if they are casual friends with God. Which way is right or wrong—or are they both OK?

In Matthew 6:9–13, we read what Jesus told His new-believer friends about prayer:

Pray, then, in this way:
"Our Father who art in heaven,
Hallowed be Thy name.
Thy kingdom come.

Thy will be done,
On earth as it is in heaven.
Give us this day our daily bread.
And forgive us our debts, as we also have forgiven our
debtors.
And do not lead us into temptation, but deliver us from
evil. [For Thine is the kingdom, and the power, and the
glory, forever. Amen.]"

Don't think of this prayer as a magic formula or some kind of mantra to keep repeating over and over; you don't have to repeat these exact words in order for God to hear you. In fact, it is much better if you use your own words, with the above prayer as an outline, as you talk to God on a regular basis.

The crucial thing to remember about prayer is this: it's not the words that matter, but the sincerity of your heart. It's that simple. God wants you to express to Him every part of who you are. He wants nothing to be in secret. When you talk to Him, tell Him about every facet of your life, every area of your personal world. He already knows everything about you, but He knows that you need to talk to Him in order to stay connected.

Prayer is an intimate experience, for Jesus says, "When you pray, go into your room, close the door and pray to your Father, who is unseen" (Matthew 6:6 NIV). He is not saying that we should never pray with other people in larger or small groups. He means that we should never pray in order to impress other people. Prayer is meant to be a personal conversation between you and the God of the universe.

Two friends who were spending the day together decided to grab some fast food for lunch. As they sat down at the table inside the crowded restaurant, one of them said, "Let me pray over the food." They both bowed their heads, and the one started to pray in a loud and religious voice, "Our Father God, we thank Thee for this meal, for the food You have provided for us." He was praying so loud that everybody in the place turned to see what was going on. In addition to thanking God for the food, he managed to work in a gospel message for the benefit of the other patrons.

The guy who wasn't praying felt like crawling under the table. It's not that he was embarrassed about his God or his faith; rather, he felt that his friend was drawing inappropriate attention to himself by praying that way in public.

When Should We Pray?

To put things in perspective, take a moment and think of a person with whom you would love to spend an entire day—somebody famous, such as a sports star, or a musician, etc. If you had that privilege, would you spend the entire day not talking to this individual? Of course not! You would talk to this person as much as you possibly could. You would ask questions about his or her personal life, where they live, what their hobbies are, where they hang out for fun, etc. There's no way you would let the opportunity pass you by without saying much to him or her.

That's how we should think about God. He is greater and more important than any sports figure, rock star, or political figure the world has ever seen. He is your constant companion—every day, all day. In your car, in your bedroom at home, in the classroom, at work—everywhere. He is always willing and ready to spend time with you and to talk with you about whatever is on your heart.

The Bible makes it clear that God is always available to us; in fact, we are commanded to pray "at all times in the Spirit" (Ephesians 6:18). That means that our conversation with God is to be continuous. Rather than just "saying our prayers" before bedtime, we are to see our life as an ongoing conversation with our heavenly Father.

The Benefits of Prayer

Karla is a girl who recently found out that her dad is having an affair and is not coming home anymore—he is abandoning her and her mom. As you can imagine, she is in total anguish, her world turned upside down like a one-thousand-piece jigsaw puzzle scattered across the floor.

When Karla talks to her friends, it helps a little. When she talks to her mom, she gets even angrier and her pain increases. And of course, she can't really talk to Dad at this point—things would just get more confusing.

She does have someone to talk to, however, who will gladly listen to her even when moans and tears replace the words that can't begin to express her pain. Somehow, as she pours out her heart to her heavenly Father, she experiences a comfort and a peace that takes the edge off of her anguish. She cries out to the Father, kneels alongside the bed, tears stinging her cheeks before dampening her pillow. She pours out her heart to the One who hears and understands. It makes a huge difference.

Over the days and weeks to follow, she survives by devouring her Bible and pouring out her soul in prayer. Her faith increases, and she finds that she can depend on God's strength, not her own, to get her through this mess. Karla finds great comfort in knowing that the God of the universe is in control of her life. He loves her, He comforts her, He guides her.

Each of us, at one time or another, will go through crises in life. It may be a family situation, as was the case with Karla, or it may be something equally difficult. Whatever the situation, you can be assured that God will walk through it with you, and He will listen to your every heart-cry.

Prayer will allow you to discern the will of God. (Look up James 1:5.) Certainly the Bible is our main source of wisdom, for in it the Father reveals to us how to live the kind of life that He will bless. Yet prayer is when much of the Bible's wisdom is confirmed to our hearts. We talk with Him, and He impresses His truth on our hearts.

Another benefit is this: through prayer we can seek forgiveness of sin. (Look up 1 John 1:9.) It's true that when you prayed to receive Christ, He paid the debt for all of your sins—past, present, and future. Those sins are no longer held against you, and they will never separate you from being eternally with the Father in heaven. Yet unconfessed sin can cause there to be a coldness in your relationship with God, just as things can come between you and any other person with whom you relate.

Sin that goes unconfessed will weigh you down. A young man named Zack hadn't spent any time alone with God for several weeks. He was ashamed of bringing the same sins to the Lord over and over again. Gradually the guilt built up until he was weighed down with a heavy spirit.

A good friend gave Zack some excellent advice. "Zack, you need to get alone with God for awhile and tell Him what's bugging you. Spend some time and pour out your heart to God."

Zack did just that, and the change in his countenance was amazing. His spirit lightened, and he felt refreshed.

When it comes to confession of sin, ask the Holy Spirit to bring to mind anything that you don't remember offhand. Psalm 19:12 says, "Who can discern [my] errors? Forgive my hidden faults" (NIV). Don't live in fear that some unforgotten sin will keep you from experiencing all that the Father has for you. Trust that He will bring to mind those things that need to be confessed.

Closing Thoughts

Perhaps by now you've heard people pray on many different occasions. If so, no doubt you've heard someone close his or her prayer by saying, "In Jesus' name, Amen." To many new Christians, this sounds kind of odd. Just what does it mean to pray "in Jesus' name"?

First off, it's not a magic formula that means one's prayer automatically gets answered. Nor is it some simple little saying that means nothing. When a person prays "in Jesus' name," it means that the person is coming to God in the authority, or name, of Jesus, His Son. Instead of coming on one's own merit, it is an acknowledgment that only Jesus makes it possible for us to approach the all-Holy God.

Prayer is to the soul what breathing is to the body. Take some time each day to talk to your Father in heaven—you may be surprised how enjoyable it can be to hold a personal conversation with God.

Small Group Discussion

1. What would happen to your spiritual walk if you prayed every day for one hour? Where would you go to pray? What would you bring with you? What is stopping you?

2. Describe your prayer life. Why would you want it to be better?

3. List some people you want to pray for today. Write out your prayers if you have a hard time concentrating.

Meditating on God's Word

Jim was never much of a reader. To him, reading a book was a chore rather than something he looked forward to.

He wasn't the kind of person who would pick up a book and read it for pleasure; even comic books weren't enjoyable. Basically the only time he would read was when it was an assignment for class, but even then he would only read the bare minimum. He would always turn the pages ahead of time in order to see how far he had to go. And when he was done, he would think to himself, *OK, what did I just read?*

Then something happened to make Jim an avid reader. It wasn't a reading course at school; it wasn't a private tutor; it wasn't even a subscription to *Sports Illustrated*. It was an experience with the living God. Jim gave his life to Christ, and for the first time ever, he found a book he had a hard time putting down—the Bible. He began to thirst after the Scriptures and the spiritual truth they contain. Instead of trying to cover lots of pages at a time, he would read at his own pace, sometimes for an hour or two without stopping. Surprisingly, the time would fly by like five minutes.

Jim found the Bible to be different from any other book he had picked up. He found that the more he read, the more fulfilled and satisfied he became. Instead of being a chore, reading actually became enjoyable for the first time in his life. Jim began to get up early in the morning so that he could find some quiet time in which to read. Each morning he would approach the Word with anticipation, excited about the things he was going to learn from his Father.

CHAPTER 24

On those mornings when he didn't feel like getting up early, he would usually push through the tiredness and get up anyway. He was always glad that he did.

Jim was amazed by the fact that the God of the universe was using words on a page to talk directly to him. Just as he would look forward to a phone call with his best friend, now it was the same with God. He felt that he was really getting to know God better and better through His Word.

Over the years since his first encounter with God's Word, Jim has become an avid seeker of truth. He still reads and rereads the Scriptures, always getting something new and fresh out of them that he hasn't seen before. His thirst to know God through the Bible has also led him to enroll in a Bible college, where he is learning more about the Bible and the Christian life than he ever thought possible. Now Jim reads several entire books alongside of the Bible each semester—something this onetime nonreader would never have imagined years ago.

Studying the Word of God is the key to one's spiritual growth. If you want to become a mature follower of Jesus Christ, you must spend time—much time—reading the Book by which He so clearly reveals Himself to us.

The Bible is unlike any other book ever written. As a Christian, the Holy Spirit who now lives in you works through the Word of God to supernaturally reveal to you the things of God. Non-Christians can read the Bible and understand some things, but they are handicapped in their ability to discern God's truth. In 1 Corinthians 2:14 it says, "But a natural man does not accept the things of the Spirit of God, for they are foolishness to him, and he cannot understand them, because they are spiritually appraised."

In the New Testament Book of Hebrews, the writer encourages readers to devour solid food, not just milk. (Look up Hebrews 5:12–14.) That is, do not remain as a baby in the faith, but grow up and mature. There's something wrong with a child who never grows up physically, and the same thing is true spiritually. God wants us to read and study His Book so that we can grow and mature as believers in Christ. And to be honest, there's no other way to reach spiritual maturity.

What the Word of God Will Do for a Believer

Let's explore this idea further by looking at four benefits of reading and studying God's Word.

1. *It will prevent us from misunderstanding who God is and what He desires for us.* No one likes to be slandered. If you've ever had someone lie about you behind your back, you know how frustrating it can be to try to recapture your reputation. In the same way, there are a lot of people who slander God by either twisting His Word or ignoring it altogether. This results in more than God getting His feelings hurt; twisted truth is the same as no truth at all, and a twisted view of God can have dire eternal consequences. God does not take this lightly.

Throughout the Old Testament, God was continually teaching the nation of Israel, His chosen people, about His character and attributes. Like us, Israel was often stubborn and rebellious in their dealings with God. One time they even rebelled against God by making a golden calf and bowing down to worship it. What a mistake! Yet we are capable of doing the very same thing if we don't allow the Bible to sharpen our spiritual focus. You may not build a golden calf, but without the Bible you will certainly fashion God into the image of something much less than He really is.

2. *The Bible gives us truth by which we can live our lives.* Imagine a steep mountain road with no guardrails. Now imagine that same road covered in ice and snow, and still no guardrails. Not a very secure feeling, is it? It wouldn't take much to slide off the edge when tragedy strikes. We all recognize that the rails are there for our safety. I don't think I've ever seen someone get mad because there are guardrails high up on mountain roads.

Yet plenty of people get mad when they understand that God is telling them how to live their lives. They don't understand that God has placed spiritual guardrails in the Bible to keep us from destroying ourselves. Those who neglect God's truth are on thin ice, spiritually speaking.

A young student named Brad was curious about the party scene at school. He had never attended a beer bash due to the fact that he was a Christian, but for some reason he felt a growing desire to attend one just to see what it was like.

Before making the final decision, however, he decided to look in the Bible to see what it had to say about parties. Though he couldn't find the words *beer* and *party*, he did find verses that said it is foolish to hang around sin. For instance, the Bible says, "My son, if sinners entice you, do not consent" (Proverbs 1:10); also, "Do not let your heart envy sinners, but live in the fear of the LORD always" (Proverbs 23:17).

As Brad meditated on these passages and others like them, his desire to attend a party began to decrease. He was still tempted, but the Word gave him the conviction and the courage to withstand the temptation. God used the Bible to keep Brad's conscience sharp. Without it, Brad could easily have made some wrong choices, possibly with lasting results.

When we read the Bible, it pulls us back to reality—God's reality. It helps us steer a course through the vain desires that would cause us to otherwise stray from His paths. Remember, God's truth exists for your safety and blessing. It acts as a guardrail to keep you from self-destruction.

3. *The Bible will keep us thirsty for the things of God.* The more you read it, the more you will *want* to read it. Unlike other books, one can never exhaust the truth in God's Word. Even if you were to read through the entire Bible twice a year for the rest of your life (which would be an awesome goal), you would never run out of things to learn. It's like a deep well that never runs dry. (Look at what it says in Ephesians 1:9.)

4. *The Word of God will give you discernment when it comes to making right choices in life—big or small.*

Ben had just entered college and was new to dorm life. That's why he was surprised during his first week of fall term when one of his roommates brought a keg of beer into the room. As the room began to fill with rowdy students, Ben had a choice to make: stay in the room with the guys or get up and leave?

Fortunately, he decided to leave, largely because his conscience had been sharpened by the Word of God. Due to his daily Bible reading, God's truth was fresh on his mind.

The Bible will help with the larger issues of life as well. For instance:

- What kind of person do you want to marry?
- How should you respond to your parents?
- Is it wrong to live with someone before you're married?
- What kind of career should you pursue?
- How do you mend relationships that have gone bad?
- Is it wrong to want to make money, or is it more godly to be poor?
- What does God think about adultery, divorce, and re-marriage?

The Bible contains great insight into each of these issues. Even though these may not be burning topics in your mind right now, someday they will be. If your mind and heart are trained by God's Word, you will have needed insight for decisions to be made at each stage of life.

Tips on How to Use the Bible

- Learn how to have devotions. Read the Bible every day.
- Write in your Bible when you want to take notes. Put a *Q* in the margin where you have a question; then ask someone about it when you have the chance.
- Take some time to study the Bible at a deeper level. Find a good study Bible (such as the *TruthQuest Inductive Student Bible*[1]) that is full of helps, notes, and maps. Find some books that will help you understand the history, geography, and culture of the time in which the Bible was written.
- One of the best tools for Bible study is the simple use of questions:
  — When was this passage written?
  — Who wrote it?
  — To whom was it written?
  — Why was this book written?

— What did it mean to the original readers?

— Are there some things I should do, or do differently, as a result of reading this passage?

- Memorize as many verses as you can. (Look up Psalm 119:11.) The best way to internalize the Word of God is to memorize it and then think about it throughout the day. You'll be amazed at how quickly your life will be changed more into Christ's image.

- Type out some favorite verses, or a whole chapter, on your computer. Print it out and place it on your car dashboard, your locker at school, or on your bathroom mirror at home.

- Write out some verses on three-by-five cards and carry them with you in your pocket or your purse. Pull them out and read them when you're standing in line somewhere and have nothing to do.

- Find a friend and read the Scriptures to each other. Take turns sharing what your favorite verses are teaching you about God.

- Buy a small pocket Bible to carry with you whenever you can. Read it during lunch break or when you find some free time.

Each of the above suggestions is designed to keep the Word of God in front of you on a regular basis. God desires to continually reveal more of Himself to you, and the primary way this happens is through His Word.

Years ago a small church in Siberia was struggling, and the members were desperate to find copies of God's Word. In such a closed country, Bibles were almost impossible to come by. In fact, many people were killed or sent to prison for the "crime" of owning a Bible.

Feeling strongly that God was speaking to them, the small church sent a man to the sprawling city of Kiev. Someone had heard that Bible smugglers from the West would sometimes unload their shipments in this big city.

After a long journey, the man arrived in Kiev. But where to look? He had no idea where to start searching, so he stopped and prayed: "Lord, lead me to some Bibles. We need them in order to know You better." He then started walking, and before long he happened upon a church. To his amazement, he learned that of all the churches in Kiev, the church he had found was the one place to which the smugglers had brought Bibles that day.

With joy the man entered the building and told of his long journey from Siberia. He told of his prayer and how the small church back home had no Bibles at all. To his surprise, he was given a whole box of Bibles to take back and share with his brothers and sisters in Christ. The man responded with tears of joy. For him, the Bible was the spiritual food for which he longed.

Don't rob yourself of this tremendous privilege by neglecting to read your Bible. It's the most precious gift God has given you besides the gift of Himself.

Small Group Discussion

1. Why do you think God gave His Word to us in written form?

2. What are the main obstacles, if any, that keep you from reading God's Word on a consistent basis? How can you overcome these obstacles?

Church

David and Kent were the best of friends. They hung out together not only at school, but they also practically lived at each other's homes. The boys were together so much that both sets of their parents thought they'd adopted another kid. These guys were really good friends.

As is often true with close friends, David and Kent spent a lot of time laughing. They were always goofing around about something. When one would start giggling, the other couldn't resist joining in. Pretty soon they would both be cracking up, tears streaming down their faces, even if what they were laughing at was dumb in the first place.

More than once, however, their quick sense of humor got them into trouble. Like the time David invited Kent to church. David was a Christian, but Kent had never expressed interest in spiritual things. That's why David was surprised when Kent said, "Sure, I'll go with you—as long as we can sit in the back."

And that's just what they did. They went on a Sunday morning and sat near the last row. David could tell that Kent was a little nervous about being there; he kept looking around at people, trying to fit in as best he could. When everybody stood up, he stood. When everyone sat down, he sat. He did his best to follow the cues.

David was aware of the church service as never before. He began to look at what was taking place through Kent's eyes, and he found himself praying more than once, "Lord, help Kent to really enjoy the service. Help him to want to come back."

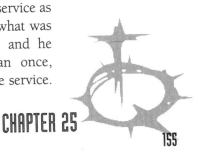

CHAPTER 25

Then "the trio" got up to sing. *Oh no,* thought David, *not the trio!* He'd heard these three ladies sing all through his growing-up years, and he'd never thought a thing about it. But now! Kent was here—what would he think?

The ladies gathered in front of the pulpit, jockeying for position in front of the microphone. These three sisters had sung more times than Elvis, but their voices had long since passed their prime. They cleared their throats in unison; then one of them looked over her shoulder and nodded knowingly at the piano player, who began the introduction to their number.

David's eyes were growing larger by the minute. He was afraid to look at Kent. As the trio began to warble, he tried to imagine what his friend was thinking. Here's three warbling sisters, singing what sounded like a German beer song with religious lyrics, while dressed in matching purple-and-yellow pantsuits that made a circus act look drab in comparison. David knew the singing sisters had great hearts; it's just that to someone from the outside it must have seemed pretty funny.

Just then David heard a muffled sound. It was coming from Kent. It was the same sound that a person makes when he catches a sneeze in the back of his throat—a gurgling noise, followed by deep breaths.

David prayed hard. He knew what it was; it was Kent trying not to snort out loud with laughter. David tried to deny the obvious.

Lord, keep us from laughing. Lord, please, help us not to break out laughing. Not now!

David turned toward Kent, and their eyes met for an instant. That's all it took. Immediately both of them were overcome with the giggles. They put their heads down and attempted to become invisible as tears rolled down their red faces. But the more they tried to stop laughing, the worse it got. By the time the song was over, they were biting their fingers—anything to distract them from laughing out loud. Thankfully, only a few people noticed the boys' heaving shoulders during the long, overdrawn song.

At the end of the service, David was sure that his friend would never want to come to church again, but Kent surprised him on the way home.

"Sure, I'll come back, as long as the three ladies are singing!" said Kent. "I'll be here next week."

Excuses

To some people, going to church can seem to get in the way of a good weekend. It's easy to find other things that seem more important when the time for church rolls around.

Do any of these excuses sound familiar?

"Church is boring."

"I don't understand the pastor; he uses too many big words."

"I don't like the music. It's for my parents, not for me."

"I don't know very many people at church; my friends are never there."

"My parents say I go to church too much. They don't go to church—why should I?"

"Church only makes me feel like a hypocrite."

"Weekends are my only days off—I'm so busy the rest of the week."

"I have to work in order to pay for my car."

It's easy to make excuses for not being at church. Be alert to excuses.

How Much Does Christ Love the Church?

Read Ephesians 5:25–27, and you will gain a picture of just how much Jesus Christ loves the church. Jesus loves the church; so much so that He paid the ultimate price for her sake—He gave His life on the cross. The Bible calls the church the "body of Christ" (1 Corinthians 12:27 NIV). It says that those who have accepted Christ into their hearts are like members of a complex and beautiful body, with Jesus Himself being the head. No wonder, then, that Jesus is so protective of the church—it is a part of Himself, and He has promised to build it and care for it until the day we are taken forever into His presence.

There is also another name for the Church: it is called the "bride of Christ." If you can imagine how a man feels about his beautiful earthly bride, just think how Christ must feel about His forever bride.

That's why it's not a good thing to rank on the church, constantly pointing out its faults in a derogatory way. Imagine if your friends were ranking on the girl you had chosen to marry. How would you feel if they constantly said things like, "She's kind of dull," or "She doesn't meet your needs."

So it is with Christ—He wants us to be proud of His body, His people. Jesus Christ is absolutely committed to His church, and He desires that we share in that same commitment.

The apostle Paul had this commitment in mind when he wrote to a small church in ancient Greece. (Look up 1 Corinthians 11:2.) Paul understood that the church is at the very center of what God is doing in our world. If we are not actively involved in a local, Bible-teaching church, then we are outside of God's plan for our lives. It's that simple.

There's no way you can be in the middle of God's will for your life if you neglect being actively involved in a local church. (Read Hebrews 10:25.)

A number of college-aged students began to get bored with the Sunday services at their small church. They couldn't get into the music and the hymns, and the pastor's sermons left them bored and uninspired.

They decided to start their own Bible study where they could read Scripture in their own way and worship with their own music. As they gathered, they found themselves complaining about the church at large. They loved just getting together and doing their own thing, and most of them began to ignore going to the regular services.

Over time, many of the students began to struggle in their walks with God. They had been fooling themselves into thinking they were active members of Christ's body. In reality, they had isolated themselves from the larger body of Christ, to their own detriment.

If you only go to the high school or college ministry of your local church, you are missing out on everything God has for you. You may not realize it, but you need to be with the church at large on a regular basis.

Many students leave the faith when they graduate from high school because they no longer feel comfortable in church. They loved the youth group, but they never became a part of the larger church body. Thus, when they graduate, they don't have a place to which they belong.

It doesn't have to be that way. A wise student will attend more than just the youth group at church. A wise student will attend worship services and find other ways to get involved. Then, as the student grows older, he or she will have a base of relationships that will carry them into a mature walk with Christ.

What the Church Provides

1. *The church provides leaders who care for you* and have responsibility to teach you and lead you in the Word of God. These leaders are recognized by the church to keep you growing in your walk with Christ.

2. *The church provides opportunities for you to meet the needs of others.* Every member of Christ's body has been given "spiritual gifts" for the purpose of serving other members of Christ's body. If you're not at church, then not only do you lose the blessing and reward of serving Christ, but the body as a whole suffers because it lacks your unique gifts and talents.

Think of how you might use your gifts within Christ's body: helping to lead worship, teaching, cleaning up, evangelizing, making hospital visits, helping with the poor, working with children, parking cars, leading Bible studies, and a million other ways that serve God. The church, when it's done right, is the most exciting place on earth.

3. *The church provides spiritual encouragement that you can find nowhere else.* It's not enough to watch church on TV each Sunday morning; Christ wants us to rub shoulders with others in His body. "Lone Ranger Christians" aren't much use when it comes to

effective ministry. Christ uses His church body to equip and prepare us for His service. (Read Ephesians 4:11–12.)

What Happens When Church Is Not a Priority

Demas was a man who worked with the apostle Paul. He started out well and appeared to love God. He was even involved in active ministry alongside Paul as churches were planted throughout the ancient world. Sadly, Demas could not resist the lure of the world. (Read 2 Timothy 4:10.)

Demas left the church. When you leave the church, you fall away from Christ. It's impossible to grow into a mature believer if church is something you do only on Christmas and Easter. Apparently, Demas thought he didn't need the church anymore. He was sadly mistaken.

A similar, yet modern-day story, is the story of Josh. He was a linebacker on his high school football team, and when he made a profession of faith in Christ, it impacted everybody on campus. Josh was so sincere about his faith that he even stood up in front of three hundred students at a retreat and shared about his love for Christ. His life was completely changed. Josh was on fire for God. He made sure his friends were with him at youth group each week, and he took great care to live a life obedient to God.

When Josh graduated, he began hanging out with the college group, but it just wasn't the same. He tried to fit in, but it was hard for him to feel comfortable. Eventually, he quit going to church altogether. He couldn't quite find a group that matched his old high school group, and when he went away to college, he didn't bother finding a new church to attend. You can guess how the story goes. Josh eventually abandoned his walk with the Lord, deciding it just wasn't worth the effort.

Josh is a good example of what happens when a person gets involved in only one ministry of the church and neglects the rest of the body.

If you're looking for a perfect church, you'll never find one here on earth. There are, however, some criteria that are important when looking for a good church home. First, make sure that it is a Bible-believing, Bible-teaching church.

Second, make sure that the church holds to the historic doctrines of the Christian faith. Some cults, such as Mormonism and Jehovah's Witnesses, claim to base their teachings on the Bible; in reality, however, they have distorted the Bible in order to teach a different Jesus. This is a crucial mistake on the part of many.

Satan wants us to think that church is going to be boring and irrelevant. Nothing could be farther from the truth. The closer you draw to Christ's body, the closer you'll draw to Him.

It's the best thing God has going in this world.

Small Group Discussion

1. What are some of the reasons that church becomes a low priority in people's lives?

2. If that's ever happened to you, what happened to your spiritual walk when you found yourself getting negative about the church? What impact does your view of church have on your friends?

The Holy Spirit

Paul loved parties. Most every day he and his friends would hang out together after school and smoke pot. On the weekends they never missed a party; to do so would be to miss their reason for living. Paul's life centered around drugs, friends, and heavy-metal music. Nothing else was really that important.

When it came to spiritual matters, Paul believed there might be a God—maybe. But he sure didn't spend much time trying to figure it out. That is until a friend invited him to church.

It wasn't like Paul to go to church. He's not sure why he said yes to the friend who invited him. Maybe he was curious to see if there were any cute girls at the youth group. Whatever the reason, that evening he was confronted with the message of the gospel for the first time. As he lay in bed that night, he couldn't get the words out of his mind. The next day he told his friend he would like to attend church the following week as well.

Step by step, Paul began to understand the message of the Bible and that he was in need of a Savior. He now understood that his life was empty and that he needed Jesus Christ to fill him with His love and forgiveness. One evening he knelt down by his bed and prayed for the first time in his life, asking Christ to come into his life.

Immediately, Paul's world was turned upside down.

He decided he didn't need drugs anymore, so he stopped hanging out with his friends after school. The more he read the Bible, the more happy he became and the less he wanted to listen to his heavy-metal CDs, so full of trash talk and death lyrics. Instead of

CHAPTER 26

going to parties on the weekends, Paul now chose to spend time with his new Christian friends, having a blast and no longer getting into trouble.

Paul's life was changing by the day, and nobody noticed it more clearly than did his family. At first his parents were convinced it was just a phase, but as the months passed by with him more and more committed to his faith, they began to take notice. Paul was still a typical teenager in many ways, but his attitude about life had changed dramatically. He was getting better grades at school, and he even spent time just sitting and talking with his folks, something he hadn't done for years. It was almost as if Paul was becoming a new person.

Paul's dad hadn't stepped foot in a church for nearly twenty years, and that time had been the first—and last—time he'd ever attended church. The sermon that day had been about money, and just as he suspected all along, the pastor's appeal for the offering was long and pushy.

"All these people want is my money," he scowled at his wife on the drive home that day. "I'm never going back there again." And for twenty years he'd kept that promise, convinced that Christianity was just a crock—until now.

The ongoing, positive changes in Paul's life were beyond anything his dad had ever seen. *Maybe there's something to this after all,* he found himself thinking in the quiet corners of his mind.

Paul's other family members were equally impacted by what they saw. His mom started going to church on a regular basis. She enjoyed it enough to invite Paul's aunt to go with her. Best of all, Paul's older sister began to attend church. In time, she and Paul's aunt both gave their lives to Christ because of Paul's strong witness. Now, both Mom and Dad have a different opinion of believers.

What happened to Paul that made his life change so dramatically? Some might say it was sheer willpower on his part, while others might conclude that it was the change of friends.

The fact is, Paul was changed because a Person came to live inside of him—the person of the Holy Spirit.

Who Is the Holy Spirit?

If you've seen any of the popular *Star Wars* movies (and let's face it—who hasn't?), then you're familiar with the "Force." The Force is a supernatural, impersonal power that Luke must tap into in order to perform spectacular feats of valor. The Force is available to anyone, yet only the Jedi knights have learned how to harness its miraculous power in order to preserve good in the universe.

Understandably, this is how many people view the Holy Spirit when they start to read the Bible. They think of the Spirit as an impersonal power, something we can tap into in much the same way that we plug an appliance into an electrical outlet. However, this is an inadequate view of the Holy Spirit for several reasons.

First, the Bible tells us that the Holy Spirit is a Person and not an impersonal force or power. In numerous places, the Holy Spirit is referred to as "He," never as an "it." He performs many acts that show Him to be a person, things such as speaking, making choices, and having a will. An impersonal force could do none of these.

Second, we learn from the Bible that He is God. The Holy Spirit is the third person of the Trinity, absolutely equal with the Father and the Son. As God, He has every attribute that is ascribed to the other members of the Godhead, such as:

- omniscience (He is all-knowing), 1 Corinthians 2:10–11
- omnipotence (He is all-powerful), Romans 8:11
- omnipresence (He is everywhere), Psalm 139:7

Only God has these qualities; thus, the Holy Spirit is fully God.

And third, the Holy Spirit is directly referred to as a part of the Trinity. (Read Matthew 28:19.)

How Does a Person Receive the Holy Spirit?

The moment a person prays to receive Christ into his or her life, the Holy Spirit takes up residence inside of them. He is there to guide, correct, and to reveal God's truth to every believer as they grow deep in the Word of God.

The Holy Spirit was sent so that you and I can experience God in the same way that the disciples experienced Jesus in the first century. This is why Jesus can promise to us what He does in Matthew 28:20: "And lo, I am with you always, even to the end of the age." He is with us by way of the Holy Spirit, who fills our hearts with God's very presence.

What Does the Holy Spirit Do?

Here are some of the primary things that the Holy Spirit does in the life of every believer.

The Holy Spirit Convicts Us of Sin

Look up 1 Corinthians 6:19.

Kendra and some friends decided to go to the movies one night. A certain movie had been recommended to them, and since it sounded interesting, they decided to drive to the theater and check it out. They paid full price for the late showing, then settled into their seats with anticipation, popcorn and sodas in hand.

Soon the lights went down and the movie filled the big screen in front of them. Kendra winced at the first scene, full of raw language that made her ears burn with embarrassment. She shrunk down in her seat, feeling uncomfortable at what was playing out in front of her.

Then a sex scene came into full view, and Kendra turned her head so as not to defile her eyes. As the scene continued to unfold, she knew that she was in a place that wasn't pleasing to her Lord. It became obvious that this was going to be a movie promoting an adulterous affair.

Kendra had seen and heard enough. She leaned over to her friends and whispered, "I'm going to wait in the lobby; I don't want to see this kind of film." She scrunched down as she scooted out of the theater, then found a bench in the lobby where she could wait for her friends. *What a bummer,* she thought to herself. She didn't like the idea of wasting seven dollars for the evening, but it was better than exposing her mind to the garbage she knew was playing on the screen.

In time, Kendra's two new-believer friends felt uncomfortable as well. They joined her in the lobby, and as they got into the car to drive home, Kendra was able to explain to her friends why the movie was inappropriate for them as Christians.

This is an example of the Holy Spirit at work. He convicts us when we are in situations that are sinful, giving us the strength to make right choices when we otherwise might compromise our purity.

The Holy Spirit Helps Us Understand the Word of God

As we study the Word of God on a daily basis, the Holy Spirit becomes our teacher, helping us to understand what the Word means. (Look up John 14:26.) The Holy Spirit will help you understand spiritual truth, truth that you couldn't have learned before you were a Christian. (Look up 1 Corinthians 2:16.)

The Holy Spirit's primary means of teaching us about God is by bringing Scriptures to our mind when we need to hear them; the more verses that you know by memory, the more He can bring to mind. The less you study God's Word, the less He has to work with.

The Holy Spirit Gives Us Guidance

Have you ever been in a situation where you've wondered what to do? Of course you have; we all reach stages of life where we wish someone would hang a sign from heaven and tell us what we should do next.

Though God doesn't usually hang any signs, He does give us the Holy Spirit to help us with guidance. (Look up Romans 8:14.)

The Scriptures tell us that the Holy Spirit will never lead us to go against what the Bible says.

Sam started dating a girl who did not know Christ. He had always been very outspoken about his Christian faith, but now he was dating a girl who did not know the Lord. They had everything in common except for their spiritual life.

Sam knew that the Bible told him that he should not date non-Christian girls (see 2 Corinthians 6:14 regarding being "unequally yoked" [NKJV]), but for some reason he felt that God was leading them to be together. His feelings told him it was OK to be in this relationship. Notice that the emphasis was on what he *felt*, not on what he knew to be true. In time the two of them moved in together, something that is completely against God's will.

The point is this: God will never be divided against Himself. The Holy Spirit will never prompt you to do something that is contrary to the Word of God. Sam didn't understand this truth, and thus ended up in an immoral situation.

The Holy Spirit Will Bear Godly Fruit in Our Lives

One of the most amazing things about the Christian life is that God does not want us to live it on our own. In fact, it's impossible to please God by being a good person in your own strength. (Read Galatians 5:16.)

Other Bible passages, such as Ephesians 5:18–21, refer to the same thing by saying, "Be filled with the Spirit." The basic meaning is the same: when you and I fill our minds and our lives with the Word of God and submit to Him the best we can, then God fills us with Himself and helps us do what we can't do on our own. (Read Galatians 5:22–23.)

Just as a pear tree produces pears and an apple tree bears apples, so the Holy Spirit will produce in you the above spiritual fruit as you consistently plant the seed of God's Word in your life.

Ask God to fill you with His Spirit on a regular basis. Keep short accounts with sin, asking God to forgive you for the things you've done wrong. Then study the Bible on a regular basis.

The Holy Spirit will be the difference between simply muddling through your Christian walk and living a power-filled, victorious Christian life that is a light for the entire world to see.

Small Group Discussion

1. In your opinion, how important is the role of the Holy Spirit in your life? Explain your answer.

2. Think of a situation when you felt God's conviction and noticed His leading in your life. How did you respond?

Notes

Chapter 3

1. Quoted in *Who Says God Created?* Fritz Ridenour, editor (Glendale, Calif.: Regal Books, 1967), 84.
2. Ibid.

Chapter 17

1. *Journal of the American Medical Association,* March 21, 1986, Volume 256.
2. Ibid.
3. Ibid.

Chapter 19

1. C. S. Lewis, *The Great Divorce* (San Francisco: Harper), 72.

Chapter 24

1. *TruthQuest Inductive Student Bible* (Nashville: Holman Bible Publishers, 1999).

Also Available

The TruthQuest™ Inductive Student Bible (NLT)
Black bonded leather with slide tab 1-55819-843-1
Blue bonded leather with slide tab 1-55819-849-0
Paperback with Expedition Bible Cover 1-55819-928-4
Hardcover 1-55819-855-5
Paperback 1-55819-848-2
Expedition Bible Cover only 1-55819-929-2

The TruthQuest™ Share Jesus without Fear New Testament (HCSB)
1-58640-013-4

The TruthQuest™ Prayer Journal
0-8054-3777-0

The TruthQuest™ Devotional Journal
0-8054-3800-9

TruthQuest™ Books
You Are Not Your Own: Living Loud for God
by Jason Perry of PlusOne with Steve Keels
0-8054-2591-8

Living Loud: Defending Your Faith
by Norman Geisler and Joseph Holden
0-8054-2482-2

Available at Your Local Book Retailer

BROADMAN
&HOLMAN
PUBLISHERS

"Fill all your gays with god"
    —Joel White